The Fabian Society

CW01099353

The Fabian Society is Britain's leading left-of-ce
political society, committed to creating the polit
debates which will shape the future of progress.... ....

With over 300 Fabian MPs, MEPs, Peers, MSPs and AMs, the Society combines the ability to influence policy debates at the highest level with vigorous grassroots debate among our growing membership of over 7000 people, 70 local branches meeting regularly throughout Britain and a vibrant Young Fabian section organising its own activities. Fabian publications, events and ideas therefore reach and influence a wider audience than those of any comparable think tank. The Society is unique among think tanks in being a thriving, democratically-constituted membership organisation, affiliated to the Labour Party but organisationally and editorially independent.

For over 120 years Fabians have been central to every important renewal and revision of left-of-centre thinking. The Fabian commitment to open and participatory debate is as important today as ever before as we explore the ideas, politics and policies which will define the next generation of progressive politics in Britain, Europe and around the world. Find out more at **www.fabian-society.org.uk**.

Fabian Society
11 Dartmouth Street
London SW1H 9BN
www.fabian-society.org.uk

 Fabian ideas
Series editor: Jonathan Heawood

First published December 2004

ISBN 07163 0613 1
ISSN 1469 0136

British Library Cataloguing in Publication data.
A catalogue record for this book is available from the British Library.

Printed in Glasgow by Bell & Bain

Family Fortunes
the new politics of childhood

edited by
Patrick Diamond
Sunder Katwala
Meg Munn

About the authors

Louise Bamfield is the lead researcher on the Fabian Commission on Life Chances and Child Poverty.

Patrick Diamond is a Special Adviser to Rt. Hon. Alan Milburn MP.

Hetty Einzig is former Research and Development Director of the Parenting Education and Support Forum.

Phil Hope is MP for Corby and East Northamptonshire, and author of *Tomorrow's Parents* and *Education for Parenthood*.

Sunder Katwala is General Secretary of the Fabian Society.

Meg Munn is MP for Sheffield Heeley and Parliamentary Private Secretary to the Minister for Children, Margaret Hodge MP. A qualified social worker, she was Assistant Director for Children's Services in York until 2000.

Sally Prentice is a public services manager and the Shadow Executive Member for Education and Children's Services in Lambeth.

Richard Reeves is an essayist for the *New Statesman* and Director of Intelligence Agency.

Mary Riddell is a columnist on *The Observer*.

Kate Stanley is Senior Research Fellow and Head of Social Policy at the Institute for Public Policy Research.

Contents

Preface

The Fabian Society has consistently played an important role in debating the most important issues and challenges facing our society, and I welcome this timely pamphlet.

As the pamphlet argues, making Britain a child-friendly society will require us to think outside the conventional image of children's issues as being nurseries and primary schools. A child-centred society will also need parent-friendly workplaces that support the ability of both mothers and fathers to have fulfilling careers and family lives—rather than having to choose between the two or endlessly juggle the competing pressures.

There are questions here for all of us, about work-life balance, about appropriate forms of childcare, and about the role of the state in supporting families. The next steps forward will be difficult, and it means listening carefully to what children and parents have to tell us about their own life experiences. That is why I particularly welcome the contribution that children and young people themselves have made to this collection.

Cherie Booth QC

Introduction: The New Politics of the Family
Sunder Katwala, Patrick Diamond and Meg Munn

C hildren and families are now more central to public debate than for many generations. This is not always to the good. Fathers in Batman suits and ferocious media wars over working mothers often generate more heat than light. But children have also moved rapidly up the public policy agenda during Labour's first two terms in office. Since 1997, the Government has appointed the first ever Children's Minister, committed a larger share of public expenditure to children's services than any other post-war government, and made its famous pledge to eradicate child poverty by 2020. 'Education, education, education' has always been central to Labour's public service reform programme and it is now widely recognised that 'investing early' is essential to any meaningful anti-poverty strategy. It has reached the point where the Conservatives have been forced to take the agenda seriously and have begun to outline their own proposals — giving the public the opportunity to examine and choose from what will be on offer at the forthcoming General Election.

This pamphlet argues that Labour can make children and families central to its public and political narrative in the way that individualism was central to Thatcherism. A modern centre-left can stake its claim to govern for the future — setting out more clearly what a 'Labour Britain' looks like after an extended period in government. We can explain what it is we want to change, and how Britain can be transformed in ways that actually mean something to millions of our fellow citizens.

The animating claim of Thatcherism was that of the hard-pressed individual being liberated from the oppressive hand of big government, legitimizing a politics of 'rolling back the state'. This was encapsulated by specific policies during the 1980s – the 'right to buy', privatization of public utilities and the promise of lower taxes (though in practice the tax take as a share of GDP rose). Thatcherism adopted a political approach based on acquisitive material individualism that 'Thatcher's children' were seen to encapsulate.

The task for Labour is to bring its policies for children and families together coherently – from addressing child poverty to ensuring new rights for children, from SureStart to effective intervention against neglect or abuse – illuminating its social democratic vision while establishing the role of enabling government in achieving this. We can shift the boundaries of political argument decisively so as to embed a new progressive consensus about the priorities and scope of government, forging a new 'common sense' for our times. This could ensure an enduring institutional and ideological legacy for Labour based on the 'opportunity society' that no future government can sweep away.

This is a highly ambitious project for a progressive party. There are hurdles and risks in undertaking it. It will require greater confidence in our ability to reshape the terms of political argument and the deeper cultural debates underlying them. As the chapters in this collection show, this requires us to address tricky moral issues about the status of the public and private realms, including the legitimacy of the state as an instrument of moral authority in the lives of children and families. There are also contentious questions about where to draw the boundaries between the state and the market, and the correct priorities for public spending.

Life chances and the politics of inequality

The 'early years' agenda has risen to prominence because of the increasing weight of evidence about its positive impact in promoting more equal life-chances. Research from US programmes shows that for every dollar invested in early years provision, $7 is saved in lower crime, better jobs and higher educational outcomes. Gosta Esping-Andersen argues that social mobility in Scandinavia is higher and social inheritance lower than Britain because for decades these countries have enjoyed universal day-care for pre-school and school-age children.[1]

The centre-left must build a child-friendly politics on the basis of its egalitarian values—based not on crude equality of outcome, but on strong equality of opportunity. A contemporary social democratic ideology cannot have moral legitimacy unless in the background it has a commitment to the equal worth of every individual. Our moral claim is that all children deserve an equal chance in life.

Louise Bamfield, lead researcher on the Fabian Society's Life Chances and Child Poverty Commission, sets out why 'Life Chances' provides the left with a resonant appeal for tackling inequality. The progress made in the five years since the target of reducing child poverty was set in 1999 has been impressive—with over 700,000 children lifted out of poverty by 2003-04. But this is the first stage, and it will become more challenging as we get to the 'hardest to reach' groups. We need a coalition of public support to secure sustained investment to tackle child poverty. The old division between the 'deserving' and the 'undeserving' poor has to be left behind if we are to ensure that every child matters.

On the global stage, public campaigns to reduce international debt and end global poverty have been strikingly successful in mobilizing a broad and deep coalition. This is set to play a crucial role in putting concerted pressure on the G8 and other governments to commit the resources necessary to meet the Millennium Development Goals. Nowhere is this global civil society campaign stronger than in Britain. Yet by contrast, there has been no public campaign of equal scale or ambition capable of ending child poverty in this generation.

3

Public spending and the role of the state

To govern is to choose. Giving priority to children and families within existing fiscal limits involves trade-offs and prioritization. In a fast-changing 'knowledge economy', the socialization of children and young people as thriving workers and citizens demands far greater reserves of parental and institutional support than ever before. If there was ever an era when families needed strong social support, it is this. Yet achieving a consensus on the left about the priorities for public investment requires an open debate about the fundamental purpose of progressive politics.

Labour has to make an explicit case for public services, public investment and a more expansive public realm. We have to make clear how this is distinct from the caricature of the top-down corporatist state of the past. Just as the modern left recognises the limits of the market in the equitable distribution of goods and services, so we have to recognise the limits of the centralised, bureaucratic state.

Yet there is a clear opportunity here for progressive politics. The 'laissez-faire right' will face a credibility gap. However much it likes to flaunt its 'pro-family' credentials, the New Right is ideologically incapable of offering concrete measures to support hard-pressed families in their daily lives.

The centre-left, however, faces hurdles of its own. Dealing with the stresses of work and family life is seen as a personal dilemma: the issues have been 'privatised' and the basic idea that we can make collective choices about the society we want is less fashionable. Sally Prentice examines what these issues mean for the provision of childcare. A universal childcare guarantee provides a 'new frontier' for the universal welfare state. It is as ambitious as the Attlee Government's commitment to universal secondary education. But with an anticipated cost of £13.5 billion, this will require both sustained public investment and a new consensus on a fair system for sharing the costs between the state, employers and citizens.

If parents want to work, the provision of childcare matters—but a child-friendly society will also need parent-friendly workplaces, which respect and cater to the twin priorities of working parents. The evidence shows that family-friendly companies are more productive and economically successful. Finland has achieved the enviable goal of becoming one of the most productive economies in the EU, combining high levels of female participation in the workforce with the EU's highest birthrates, through an enduring consensus of support for families.

Richard Reeves, however, is surely right to argue against a view that it is always possible to have the best of all progressive worlds. The centre-left must sustain its hard-fought reputation for economic competence, while digging deeper into the issue of how we govern markets. A contrasting viewpoint is provided by Mary Riddell, who believes that the Labour Government has not gone far enough on children's rights. However, the campaigners she quotes in evidence failed to gain real resonance with the wider public or significant support from MPs during the progress of the Children Act.

Why the left needs a new politics of the family

Many families today experience huge strain. Relationships are breaking down at a rapid rate, and more children are growing up in disrupted families. There is a direct public policy interest here. Weakened families cost the state money both directly and indirectly and as such the state has a public interest in strengthening families, regardless of their structure. Families are the foundation of civil society, where we first learn moral values. Families generate social capital—the trust and relationship skills that enable individuals to co-operate.

The left finds it easy to talk about children but difficult to discuss families. Yet families have a greater impact on childhood development and life chances than any other factor. We must have the confidence to debate these issues openly and reshape the politics of the family. Ironically, it has been parties of the centre-left, not the centre-right, that have led the way in thinking about ways to stabilize family life. They have done so without taking the moral high-ground, while avoiding nostalgia for the past — no mean feat in the history of family policy.

While the left should respond sceptically to fantasies of a 'golden age' of the traditional family, we have shyed away from acknowledging the importance of two parents for children's life chances — despite the strength of the evidence. Supporting families to cope with the stresses of everyday lives is important in helping parents to put their children first and a new politics of the family should aim to strengthen families disrupted by divorce or breakdown, with children's well-being at the heart of policy. Families matter and the state cannot simply compensate for their absence.

Public and media debate remains polarized around the question of what type of families we want. But as Kate Stanley argues in chapter one, it would be more productive to focus on how public policy should best respond to the empirical evidence — how we best support the families we've got. The social revolution in the position of women is permanent. Only an extreme fringe minority in our society want to turn back the clock.

A larger number may feel discomfited by the fact that more than four in ten births in Britain now occur outside wedlock. But policymakers need to deal with the world as it is. Despite some evidence of the renewed popularity of marriage it is difficult to envisage any credible strategy to reverse this trend that does not transgress the values of an open society. A progressive politics of the family can clearly see the inherent limitations of endorsing one single family type to the exclusion of others.

The family is, rightly, the most private and jealously guarded of social institutions. So a new progressive politics of the family must concern itself with autonomy and opportunity — how families and individuals can live their own lives to the full. We have to respect, and to be seen to respect, that deep-held sense of autonomy while also demonstrating that the state does have a legitimate, and essential, role in enabling people to exercise choice. Our passion is improving people's control over their own lives.

The centre-left must unstick itself once and for all from the quagmire of 'nanny state' rhetoric. The lesson for the future is a simple one. Governments should focus on valuing families, strengthening and stabilizing them in all shapes and sizes, but not moralizing about them. Phil Hope's chapter provides compelling evidence from a variety of programmes that encourage and foster effective fathering. Those who experience these programmes find them enriching and life-enhancing.

Attention will focus increasingly on the father's role in family life, forcing issues such as paid parental leave to the top of the public agenda. Effort might also be directed at low-income non-resident fathers through New Deal schemes that integrate personal and social skills training. Evidence to date from various innovative schemes in the USA suggests that such programmes have wide appeal both for their employment and educational component, provided that participation is not forced on fathers.

As Kate Stanley argues: 'the evidence shows that parenting is too important to ignore and intervention need not be intrusive.' Hope proposes that constructive interventions should focus on the key 'transition points' in the lives of children, young people and families. More 'carrots' would rebalance the debate in favour of positive incentives.

The challenge for governments in the twenty-first century is to find ways to stabilise families in an era of globalisation, and to enhance child-rearing capacity, without imposing unsustainable burdens on taxpayers and the state. The time is ripe for a progressive child-centred family policy that acknowledges new realities and affirms enduring values.

References

1. Esping-Anderson, G., *The Welfare State in Post-Industrial Economies* (Oxford: Clarendon, 1999).

1 | Britain 2005: The Families We've Got

Kate Stanley

I've learned from being small what's right and wrong and if it's similar to what I know is right it's often right

Helen, 13

Children have been given prominence within the Labour Government's policy priorities. The Prime Minister Tony Blair has made a historic commitment to end child poverty within a generation and the Labour Party has been described by one commentator as 'the children's champion'.[1] The Government is spending more on children than ever before: there has been a 53 per cent rise in real terms in child-contingent support since 1999 and this trend is set to continue.[2] But the priority awarded to children by the Labour Government since 1997 does not in itself amount to a child-centred politics. If all children are to thrive and fulfil their potential in a just society, there is much work still to be done and many trends are heading in the wrong direction.

The experiences of children will influence both their individual well-being and our collective future as a society. This does not mean taking a deterministic view, whereby poor early experiences seal the fate of a child, but it is about identifying the policies that can bring hope for those children born into disadvantage. Moreover, childhood is important in its own right. We should be concerned with life experiences as much as life chances.

Although certain family types tend to be associated with chronic drivers such as poverty and unemployment, there is increasing evidence that it is the quality of care and not the way it is arranged that matters most for children. There is a need to focus on the role of the family, rather than how it is structured, and on allocating resources to those most poorly equipped to cope. The extent to which a fairer society can be achieved in the future depends on the extent to which mechanisms to reduce child poverty can be rooted in the fabric of public policy. The elimination of child poverty will make it easier for children to escape the cycle of deprivation, and will expand opportunities throughout society. This also means giving parents more support and time to focus on parenting. Notwithstanding concerns about overstepping the legitimate boundaries of the state, there are clear opportunities for public policy to support parents in their caring role, and to protect their children from high-risk activities, particularly in terms of health and anti-social behaviour.

This chapter outlines the key trends and drivers of change affecting children and family life that should inform the development of any child-centred policies, with particular focus on five key areas: changing families, child poverty, social mobility, health and anti-social behaviours and parenting.

Changing families

The profile of Britain's families is changing rapidly. We are having fewer children and there is a wider range of family structures. These changes present both challenges and opportunities for embedding a progressive future. Britain has an ageing population. Between 2004 and 2050, the number of people aged 20 to 64 will remain at just over 35 million, whilst the number of people aged 65 and over is forecast to increase by 79 per cent to almost 17 million.[3] One of the implications of this trend is that today's children will need to be more productive when they reach working age, as there will be fewer of them to support a larger retired population. This is a strong argument for child-centred policies that invest in children. However, it is a mistake to think of children just as the workers of tomorrow. Child-centred politics should also recognise childhood as valuable to individuals, families and communities in its own right, and regard children as citizens of the present as well as the future.

The ageing of the population is the result of a combination of increasing longevity and declining birth rates. The birth rate in the UK has been below replacement level since the 1970s.[4] This is related to increases in the educational attainment of women. Women with higher educational qualifications tend to have children later than those without.[5] There is a causal relationship between the age of a woman at the birth of her first child and the number of children she has; the older she is, the fewer children a woman is likely to have.[6] The consequence is that more highly educated women, who tend to be in higher socio-economic classes, tend to have fewer children. In addition, there is a substantial pay penalty to becoming a mother in the UK, with mothers earning, on average, 12.6 per cent less than their female counterparts without children.[7] Both these trends could exacerbate existing economic inequalities and increase the need to support families with children.

The 'nuclear family' of two parents and their children continues to be the norm in statistical terms but other family arrangements have become increasingly common in recent decades.[8] There has been a considerable increase in the number of lone parent families, with a quarter of all children now living in one.[9] Five times as many children are being born outside marriage as 30 years ago, with 40 per cent of all live births in 2001 being to unmarried mothers.[10] But the fastest growing family arrangement is the stepfamily. Divorce rates have doubled in the last 30 years, and around 40 per cent of children now experience divorce in their family before they are 16.[11]

Like all family arrangements, both lone parent families and stepfamilies present challenges for public policy. Lone parents are consistently poorer than couple families. One third of all children living in poverty in 2003 lived in lone parent households.[12] This is partly accounted for by the relatively low employment rate of lone parents (47 per cent compared to 93 per cent of couple families with at least one parent in work).[13] The growth in stepfamilies points to a strong trend towards social rather than biological parenting. At the same time the role of separated biological parents cannot be ignored.

Explanations for the changes in family types over the last 30 years are prone to caricature. There is a tendency, particularly on the right, to cite these trends as evidence of moral decline. Then there are those, particularly on the left, who cite the same trends as evidence of 'self-actualisation' and 'democratisation', whereby individuals have become freer to choose to end unfulfilling relationships and enter new ones, creating more equal and mutually satisfying relationships within the family and between genders.[14] Public policy must be based on a more sophisticated understanding of the family than either of these caricatures. There are two key dimensions to understanding family change that must underpin future public policy. Firstly, empirical evidence supports the idea that it is the quality of care and not its arrangement that matters most. This means that public policy needs to move away from a focus on the social institution of the family and towards a focus on the role of the family—in other words, we need a focus on what the family does, rather than what it is.[15] Secondly, there is a growing recognition that there are real differences in the way that people cope with changes in their family arrangements, and there is consequently a need to allocate resources to support those who are coping least well.

Child poverty

The rates of child poverty in the UK during the 1980s and 90s were of grave concern. In 1998 the UK had the highest level of child poverty in Europe. It is well established that persistent poverty during childhood has significant scarring effects on life chances. It also has dramatic impacts on the immediate experiences of children.

Good progress has been made and it is likely that the government will succeed in reaching its target of reducing child poverty by a quarter by 2004. Nonetheless, in 2002/03, 23 per cent of children still lived in households earning below 60 per cent of median income. Making further progress on child poverty is likely to become increasingly challenging, requiring bolder policies. In order to halve child poverty it has been suggested that the government would need to spend an additional one per cent of Gross Domestic Product on child tax credits, or achieve a substantial rise in rates of parental employment, particularly among lone parents.[16] There are areas where very little progress has been made through the current approach; for example, there has been no progress on the numbers of children living in overcrowded or inadequate accommodation, which can have negative impacts on children's health, behaviour and educational attainment.[17] Similarly, little attention has been paid to wealth inequality, which has a particular importance in the lives of children because this is how they experience difference in relation to their peers. Inequality in disposable income (after taxes and benefits) appears to have increased slightly since 1997.

Social mobility

Delivering social mobility is about giving children the chance of better outcomes. Social mobility is a measure to describe the extent to which people move between groups during their lifetime, moves which bring advantages and disadvantages in terms of employment, income, education, crime, housing and quality of life. In the UK, poor social mobility means that children who grow up in low-income households are likely to earn lower wages as adults.[19] Between 1972 and 1992, social mobility increased very gradually before declining slightly in the period up to 1997.[20] This low level of social mobility is not inevitable; in recent decades social mobility has increased in countries such as France, Sweden and the Netherlands.

Research shows that the key factors influencing social mobility are the quality of early childhood experiences, such as childcare, and education. Just six months after birth, class differences in childhood cognitive development can be clearly seen, and by the age of six the child with low cognitive ability from the wealthy family has already overtaken the poor but clever child.[21] Such evidence demonstrating the importance of early experiences to life chances has led to an increasing policy focus on the early years, with investment in childcare and early years services such as SureStart. The policy focus to date has generally been on the availability, quality and cost of childcare, but it is likely that future debate will also centre around the type of childcare available, in light of growing evidence that institutional settings may be inappropriate for very young children.[22]

For early interventions to have a lasting impact, the momentum must be maintained into later childhood, particularly during key transitions.[23] Early years investments by themselves, though important, are unlikely to reduce the effects of childhood disadvantage on children's adult outcomes.[24] Identifying effective ways to sustain the impact of early years intervention is an impending policy challenge. Education is one way of maintaining the momentum of the early years, as it can weaken the association between class origins and class destinations, and enhance social mobility.[25] However, stark class-driven inequalities between schools and children's attainment persist. Primary school results are improving, but schools with more children eligible for free school meals have made less progress than schools with a less deprived intake, although on other measures the gap is narrowing.[26] The number of pupils leaving school with no qualifications is falling, but 23 per cent of children receiving free school meals gained five or more GCSEs grade A to C compared to 54 per cent of all children. By age 21, just 15 per cent of young people from unskilled social backgrounds begin higher education compared with 79 per cent of young people from a professional background.[27]

So whilst there has been some progress in creating the early years and educational infrastructure required to boost social mobility in Britain, the kind of radical shift in trends that is needed to change the life chances of the poorest children is still a long way off.

Unhealthy and antisocial behaviour

The coming years are likely to see a further increase in attention on problematic childhood behaviours. In a 2004 survey of 35 countries, worryingly high levels of risky behaviour were found among UK teenagers.[28] Whilst comparable countries such as the US and the Netherlands have seen a steadying or decrease in behavioural problems, a recent study has found that adolescent conduct problems in the UK have shown a continuous rise for both boys and girls since 1975.[29] Longitudinal studies have found that the most important childhood predictors for future offending include anti-social behaviour in childhood, poor school attainment, family poverty and poor parenting.[30] These risk factors make plain the importance of early intervention to tackle disadvantage.

Class driven health inequalities in Britain are stark. For example, infant mortality rates in low-income areas are around 70 per cent higher than in the most affluent areas and a baby boy born to parents in the professional classes can expect to live over seven years longer than one born into the bottom social class.[31] Responding to such inequalities has become a priority for public policy and has helped direct the focus on early years. Attention has also been turning towards problematic behaviours affecting health during later childhood, where there are increasing levels of obesity, rates of sexually transmitted infections and mental health problems. The explanations for these worrying trends are far from clear and the public policy tools under-developed at best. For example, in the decade to 2001, the number of new episodes of sexually transmitted infections reported at clinics rose by 143 per cent. Young people are particularly vulnerable to poor sexual health as a result of high-risk sexual behaviour, but the most effective interventions to change that behaviour are not well established or resourced.[32] Interventions have helped reduce teenage conception rates by almost 10 per cent since 1998, but Britain's teenage pregnancy rate continues to be the highest in Western Europe.[33]

Adolescent emotional problems such as depression and anxiety appear to have increased for both boys and girls since the mid 1980s.[34] Evidence suggests that these increases are not attributable to changes in thresholds for what counts as a problem (that is, they are not the result of an increasing tendency for parents to rate teenagers as problematic), but are the result of real changes in problem levels. There is a relationship here to rising levels of self harm and drink and drug abuse.

Parenting

Research has consistently shown the critical importance of parents to children's outcomes, and policy has begun to turn its attention here. One comprehensive review found that parents had seven times more influence on child outcomes than the next most influential factor.[35]

There are clear opportunities for public policy to support parents in their caring role. Evidence has revealed growing dissatisfaction among parents – particularly mothers – about their ability to balance their caring and working responsibilities. The proportion of female employees dissatisfied with the balance between their work and non-working lives grew from just over a quarter in 1992 to over half in 2000.[36] This dissatisfaction may reflect higher parental expectations, for parents report spending three times as much times per day with their children as they did 30 years ago.[37] There is a role for public policy to intervene to help reconcile the interests of business and the family in a way that recognises the critical importance of parents' dual role as workers and carers.

As the traditional 'breadwinner' model of family has gradually been replaced by the 'adult worker' model of family, the role of fathers has and will come under increasing scrutiny. Evidence has shown that engaged fathers can bring emotional and psychological benefits to their children. Policy will need to find new ways to ensure fathers can participate in their children's lives, whether they live with them or not, and

15

this will mean reconciling the demands of work and care. Women continue to do the majority of care work, whilst fathers in the UK on average work longer hours than their contemporaries in the rest of Europe. Nearly three quarters of fathers work over 40 hours a week and 14 per cent work over 60 hours a week.[38] Fathers with dependent children tend to work even longer hours than non-fathers.[39]

Despite the profound impact that the parent-child relationship has on a child's development, parenting had been under-acknowledged in public policy until recent investment in the Parenting Fund, Parentline Plus and the greater involvement of parents of children in the criminal justice system. The evidence shows that parenting is too important to ignore and that intervention need not be intrusive.

Conclusion

Families in Britain are changing. These changes bring opportunities for individuals less constrained by convention, but there are attendant risks, such as the higher prevalence of poverty among lone parent families. Child-centred policy has the greatest potential if it concentrates on the function of families, not their structure. This means supporting the caring role of families through parenting support, and giving families the means to ensure that children do not grow up in poverty. There has been progress in these areas but the challenges ahead look even greater as child poverty becomes harder to tackle and society struggles to establish the most appropriate boundaries between the role of the family and that of the state.

There is some reason to be confident that the recent policy focus on early years and education will bring greater social mobility and enable every child to fulfil their potential in the years to come. But whilst there has been considerable progress in bringing children to the centre of policy making, there is still a long way to go before all children have the opportunity to fulfil their potential. The trends on behavioural problems and child mental health are worrying. Further progress will require substantial political commitment and resources.

References

1. Toynbee, P., 'New Labour is the children's party – so why are they so afraid of championing the smacking ban?' *The Guardian* (July 2, 2004).

2. Adam, S., and Brewer, M., *Supporting Families: The Financial Costs and Benefits of Children Since 1975* (Bristol: The Policy Press, 2004); HM Treasury Budget (2004).

3. Banks, J., Emmerson, C. and Oldfield, Z., 'Not so brief lives' in *Seven Ages of Man and Woman. A look at life in Britain in the Second Elizabethan Era* (Swindon: ESRC, 2004).

4. The number of births per woman needed to keep the population at the same level (excluding migration).

5. Lutz, W., Scherbov, S., Sanderson, W., 'The end of world population growth', *Nature*, 412 (2001), 490-1.

6. Esping-Andersen, G., *Progressive Governance Conference* (London, 2003).

7. Harkness, S., and Waldfogel, J., *The Family Gap in Pay: Evidence from Seven Industrialised Countries* (London: Centre for Analysis of Social Exclusion, 1999).

8. Ferri, E., Bynner, J., and Wadsworth M., (eds.) *Changing Britain, Changing Lives* (London: Institute of Education, 2004).

9. Department for Work and Pensions (2003). This figure varies across ethnic groups—for example, almost half the Black Caribbean babies in the Millennium Cohort Study lived in lone parent families. See Dex, S., and Joshi, H., *Millennium Cohort Study First Survey: A User's Guide to Initial Findings* (London: Centre for Longitudinal Studies, 2004).

10. Barrett, H., *UK Family Trends 1994-2004 Executive Summary* (London: National Family and Parenting Institute, 2004).

11. Office of National Statistics (2004).

12. Department for Work and Pensions (2003).

13. *Ibid.*

14. Williams, F., *Rethinking Families* (London: Calouste Gulbenkian Foundation, 2004).

15. *Ibid.*

16. Institute for Fiscal Studies (2003).

17. Shelter, *Living in Limbo, Surveys of Homeless Households Living in Temporary*

Accommodation (London, 2004).

18. Paxton, W., and Dixon, M., *The State of the Nation: An Audit of Injustice in the UK* (London: IPPR, 2004).

19. Blanden, J., Goodman, A., Gregg, P., and Machin, S., 'Changes in Intergenerational Mobility in Britain' in Corak M. (ed.), *Generational Income Mobility in North America and Europe* (Cambridge: Cambridge University Press, 2004).

20. Payne, G., and Roberts, J., 'Opening and Closing the Gates: Recent Developments in Male Social Mobility in Britain', Sociological Research Online, 6 (2002).

21. Feinstein, L., 'Not Just the Early Years: The Need for a Developmental Perspective for Equality of Opportunity', *New Economy* 10:4 (December 2003).

22. Waldfogel, J., 'Social Mobility & The Early Years', HM Treasury Conference on Social Mobility (London: Columbia University & CASE, 2004).

23. 'Not Just the Early Years'.

24. *Ibid.*

25. Aldridge, S., 'The Facts about Social Mobility', *New Economy* 10:4 (2003).

26. Office of the Deputy Prime Minister, *Tackling Social Exclusion: Taking Stock and Looking to the Future* (London: ODPM, 2004). Free school meals are used as a proxy for deprivation.

27. Iacovou, M., and Berthoud, R., *Young People's Lives: A Map of Europe* (Colchester: Institute for Social and Economic Research, 2001).

28. Currie, C., *et al*, *Health Policy for Children and Adolescents* (Copenhagen: World Health Organisation, 2004).

29. Collishaw, S., Maughan, B., Goodman, R., and Pickles, A., 'Time Trends in Adolescent Mental Health', *Journal of Child Psychology and Psychiatry*, 45 (November 2004).

30. McCarthy, P., Laing, K., and Walker, J., *Offenders of the Future? Assessing the Risk of Children and Young People Becoming Involved in Criminal or Antisocial Behaviour* (London: DfES, 2004).

31. Department of Health, *Tackling Health Inequalities: Summary of the 2002 Cross-Cutting Review* (London: HMT/DoH, 2002).

32. Office of National Statistics (2004).

33. *Re-integrating Teenage Parents Back into Education* (London: Department for Education and Skills, 2004).

34. 'Time Trends in Adolescent Mental Health'.

35. *Re-integrating Teenage Parents Back into Education.*

36. *Working in Britain in 2000* (2002).

37. *Rethinking Families.*

38. *Ibid.*

39. Equal Opportunities Commission, Fathers Direct and Fawcett Society joint press release (2004).

2 | Life Chances: The New Politics of Equality
Louise Bamfield

When I am older I want to be a footballer or an armed policeman.

Alex, 9

The language of life chances is set to transform the way we talk about social justice in Britain, because rather than focusing on inequality of outcome, or making exclusively socialist arguments in favour of state-sponsored redistribution, the concept of life chances deliberately appeals to a wider sense of fairness, bringing together people from across the political spectrum. The idea of life chances captures the universal revulsion we feel when asked to imagine two babies lying side by side in a maternity ward, delivered by the same doctors and midwives, yet with completely different lives ahead of them. Gordon Brown developed the idea of life chances in his 2004 speech to Labour Party Conference when he decried the fact that a poor child is still three times more likely to die before the age of one than a child born into privilege. Almost everyone would agree that all children should have the best chance in life.

At a time when the boundary between the state and the individual is ever more hotly contested, the concept of life chances provides a refreshing and convincing way forwards. A society which accepts that all children should be afforded the same opportunities must, surely, sign up to the new progressive consensus? Unfortunately, it's not that easy. There are important issues to be resolved in our interpretation and implementation of the concept of life chances before we can devise a coherent set of strategies. How can the state intervene effectively to maximize everyone's life chances, without eroding individual liberties? What imbalances are we able to rectify, and what must we leave to fate? And what exactly do we mean by 'life chances' anyway?

It is to find answers to these questions, and to examine ways of improving the life chances of disadvantaged children, that the Fabian Society has set up a Commission on Life Chances and Child Poverty.[1] The Commission's work on life chances promises to dispel complacency about the state of social justice in this country, as the full scale of the trend towards increased inequalities of wealth, income and power which occurred in the 1980s and 90s becomes apparent. Despite the Commission's timeliness, however, it is not always clear what the concept of life chances adds to debates on equality and social justice. The purpose of this chapter is to offer that clarification.

What are life chances?

The concept of life chances encapsulates the idea that children born into families in different social positions have markedly different prospects, both for achieving certain outcomes in adulthood and enjoying valuable developmental experiences throughout their lives.

By 'life chances' we mean the likelihood or probability of children from different social and ethnic backgrounds achieving certain outcomes at successive stages of the life course and across generations. Children born into families in different social positions have widely differing prospects across a range of dimensions — health, housing, environmental quality, education and employment — which all have a direct impact on wellbeing and quality of life.

In its starkest terms, differences in the life chances of people in different social class positions are illustrated by marked variations in life expectancy: men in unskilled social classes die on average 7.4 years earlier than their counterparts in professional social classes, while women in unskilled social classes die on average 5.7 years earlier.[2]

In addition, children from professional and managerial backgrounds are statistically far more likely to experience higher levels of physical and cognitive development than those from unskilled manual working class backgrounds. Marked inequalities exist between the learning opportunities open to children in 'higher' and 'lower' social positions, which translate into vastly different employment and life opportunities as adults.

Take, for example, the life chances of equally talented and equally energetic children from different social backgrounds—say, the son of a corporate accountant and the daughter of an office cleaner. In many respects—where they live, where they shop, where they go to school—we can imagine the children of a cleaner and an accountant living essentially parallel lives.

As a result of the more extensive learning experiences and opportunities for development afforded by his privileged background, which include attending a school with better qualified teachers, the accountant's son has a greater chance of gaining the requisite academic qualifications that grant entry into further and higher education institutions.[3] In addition, he will ultimately have a far greater chance of finding fulfilling employment—that is, of having a career which offers rewarding work and prospects of personal development, rather than being forced to take a job—any job—to get by.

Just as importantly as any future outcome, the quality of their experiences as they grow up is markedly different: the well-being and happiness of the cleaner's daughter is affected by physical aspects of her childhood, such as the environmental quality of the local area and housing stock, as well as her feelings of physical safety and security.

By the time they are six years old, children from disadvantaged backgrounds who demonstrated higher ability as infants have been overtaken by children from more affluent backgrounds who demonstrated lesser ability.[4] This offends against our conviction that children should be rewarded according to their talents and effort, rather than allowing their outcomes to be determined by factors beyond their control, such as family background.

What troubles us about the marked disparities in the experiences and opportunities of different children is that children's life prospects are determined by contingencies of social fortune—a mere accident of birth—rather than by natural ability. Our sense of unfairness arises from the belief that social origin is morally no less arbitrary a determinant of educational, occupational and other outcomes than discrimination on the grounds of skin colour or religious belief.

What concerns us, moreover, is not merely the fact that *talented* children from income-poor backgrounds are less likely to realise their potential than those from affluent families, but that *all* children from income-poor backgrounds are less likely to realise their potential, and to live in meaningful and rewarding ways than children from affluent families.

There is a useful business case to be made for tackling poverty and lack of opportunity: we might highlight, for instance, the impact that material deprivation and its attendant problems has on the rest of society, in terms of the public cost of welfare and income support, the cost in lost earnings of non-participation in education, employment or training, the costs incurred through wasted talent, or the cost of future medical and social care as a result of the long-term impact on people's mental and physical health.

But arguably the reason it matters—or ought to matter—to every member of society is that poverty denies the equal moral worth of every citizen. Poverty corrodes the lives of people who experience it, in its effects on their psychological and physical health, and also because it affects their ability to live in meaningful and rewarding ways. In particular it denies their right to self-respect, the most basic of all goods. Without self-respect, nothing that we do can have meaning for us. The social bases of self-respect include both objective conditions, such as the material circumstances that enable us to develop and pursue our aspirations, and subjective conditions, such as a social environment which allows us to associate with other people in mutually affirming ways. It is precisely this kind of self-respect that children and adults living in poverty are denied when they are treated in disrespectful, belittling or humiliating ways.

It follows that a genuinely inclusive society is one that considers the development of people with less innate ability to be as important as fulfilling the potential of those with greatest 'natural' talent. This suggests problems with an interpretation of social mobility as 'sponsored' mobility, based on the ostensibly meritocratic principle that children with greatest 'merit' deserve the greater material rewards in terms of income, assets and status that are attached to higher social positions, or that people with greatest marketable skills deserve higher pay and more rewarding career opportunities.

The goal, in other words, is not simply to help talented children from poor backgrounds progress up the social ladder, and so have access to a broader range of goods and opportunities than their less-talented peers, but to challenge the very existence of an exclusive and divided society, in which access to public goods such as health and education depends on one's social position.

A truly decent society is one which aspires towards a fair allocation of resources for the development of all children's capacities. A genuinely inclusive society also recognises that children with learning difficulties or physical disabilities may have special educational needs, which require additional funding. A 'fair' allocation of resources for the development of people's capacities is not therefore equal in a mathematical sense; but is 'equal' insofar as it respects the equal moral worth of every person and their equal right to the development of individual capacities.

The good society, moreover, is one which insists that the contribution people make to society should not be measured solely in terms of market value: as Polly Toynbee demonstrates in *Hard Work: Life in Low-Paid Britain*, people who undertake vital but low status work, such as

cleaning, receive only meagre wages and unsatisfactory working conditions despite their extraordinary effort and personal sacrifices. What is
needed, then, is a rethinking of the way that 'merit' and 'contribution'
are understood, to reflect the contribution that people in all social positions make to the life of the community and good of society, regardless
of their purely financial 'worth'.

What can be done to address uneven life chances?

Uneven life chances start in childhood. Therefore it is to the conditions
in which children are brought up and the opportunities available to
them as they develop that we must look to alleviate the continued existence of inequalities in our society.

What would be required to achieve a genuinely inclusive society, in
which children from disadvantaged social backgrounds enjoyed equal
life chances in core areas such as health and education? It would mean
addressing inequalities that arise before children start school—and
indeed, before they are even born—which means attending to the early
years agenda of improved parenting skills to foster child development,
as well as promoting the health of prospective mothers and physical
development of infants. In addition to a focus on the early years, we
would need to identify the appropriate policy interventions at key tran-
sitional periods, notable amongst which are the move from primary to
secondary education and the transition from school or college into
further and higher education, training and employment.

The Fabian Commission on Life Chances and Child Poverty is
concerned about the fact that that even though the Government is ambi-
tiously trying to address child poverty and has made good progress
towards that aim, vast inequalities of life chances, income, wealth and
power remain between people from different social backgrounds.[5]

The Commission has identified a range of dimensions across which
life chances are explored, which include health, education, occupation,
safety and security, social networks, personal autonomy, respect and
self esteem. These dimensions give a clear statement of what it is that

25

every child is entitled to, and what is missing from the lives of children in poverty. Part of the work of the Commission will be to evaluate the Government's programme of policy measures to tackle child poverty and to identify gaps in current provision.

To break the cycle of disadvantage, moreover, we need first to understand the processes and causal mechanisms by which advantage and disadvantage are transferred over time, across generations and over the course of an individual's life. To this end, the Commission is undertaking statistical analysis to investigate causal mechanisms, which will help to clarify the requisite policy interventions.

Any analysis into what can be done must take into account the difficulties of finding effective and legitimate ways to intervene in those processes. Part of the difficulty is that some of the processes and mechanisms by which advantage is transferred are not in themselves objectionable. Whatever our views on the independent school sector, for example, we can see the absurdity of objecting to parents assisting their children's development in less material ways—through basic acts of good parenting, such as encouraging them to read widely and involving them in discussions around the dinner table. Conversely, we do not consider children to be seriously disadvantaged when their parents drive less expensive cars, but it is worrying if children of income-poor parents do not have access to an affordable and reliable public transport system—a real risk in many deprived parts of the country. Transport has obvious implications for the quality of children's experiences, affecting, for example, their ability to take advantage of leisure services. Holidays are another moral grey area; the children of professionals and the super-rich may enjoy numerous holidays in far-flung places every year, but whilst we might be concerned if the cleaner's daughter were denied any kind of holiday at all, differences in holiday destinations are not in themselves morally objectionable.

While few would argue that irrelevant factors such as class, ethnicity and gender should be allowed to influence people's access to goods and opportunities, it is far more controversial to assume that contingencies of social fortune should be nullified, if by this we mean transforming social structures to remove 'undeserved' sources of advantage. To explain how a fairer society can legitimately be achieved we need to find ways to compensate children from income-poor families for the disadvantages they face, whilst recognising the necessary limits to state action to remove all sources of disadvantage.

In addition, ways need to be found to rectify inadequate health and social care services in parts of the country, particularly on the 88 worst estates, as well as addressing the problems that lead to low take-up of services that are available. Public and social services must find ways of connecting with families in the most disadvantaged social groups, which includes those who are lone parents, who lack educational qualifications and occupational skills, who are disabled, who live in areas where jobs are scarce, or who are members of certain ethnic minority groups, especially Pakistanis and Bangladeshis. Connecting with the hardest to reach groups is not always facilitated by competition for funds by a plethora of agencies.

Most importantly of all, we need to find ways of communicating our belief in the moral and political importance of tackling poverty and inequality to a wider range of people and of making the case for sustained investment and reform. To win the political argument, we need to do more than list the disparities in the life chances of children from different backgrounds: we need first to understand the sense of unfairness that people feel about particular kinds of inequality and to find the language which resonates best with different groups of people. This is something which the Fabian Commission is exploring in its current work, the findings of which will be published in an interim report in February.

References

1. The Fabian Commission on Life Chances and Child Poverty was launched in March 2004. It is chaired by Lord Adebowale and consists of the following members: Fran Bennett, Ruth Cadbury, Richard Exell, Ruth

Lister, David Piachaud, Aftab Rahman, Andrew Robinson, Peter Townsend and Polly Toynbee.

2. Office for National Statistics (2002). These figures relate to the years 1997-1999.

3. In 2000, children with parents in unskilled manual occupations were only half as likely to get five or more GCSEs grade A*-C as children with parents in professional/managerial occupations. See *Statistical First Release, Youth Cohort Study: The Activities and Experiences of 16 year olds: England and Wales* (DfES, 2003). The figures for 1991 are even more striking, when children with parents in professional/managerial occupations were four times as likely to get five or more GCSEs grade A*-C than children with parents in unskilled manual occupations, showing that while social-class gradients have persisted in the 1990s, inequalities in educational attainment have decreased.

4. Feinstein, L., 'Inequality in the Early Cognitive Development of British Children in the 1970 Cohort', *Economica*, 20 (2003), 73-97.

5. The Government is widely believed to have reached its first target of reducing child poverty by a quarter by 2004/05. But it is expected to encounter increasing difficulties in reaching the target of reducing child poverty by a half by 2010 and eradicating child poverty by 2020, because it must find ways of helping the hardest to reach families.

3 | Providing Universal Childcare
Sally Prentice

I went to a childminder when I was about three years old. It's probably okay for a short time but not for the whole of your childhood.

Fergus, 14

The provision of universal, high-standard childcare is one of the biggest challenges facing this country. The Government needs to build on the success of SureStart by developing childcare services for all families in every neighbourhood, if it is to achieve its target of abolishing child poverty by 2020 and provide greater help to parents balancing the demands of work and family life.

The political priority for a third term Labour Government must be to provide after-school childcare and holiday programmes for children aged three to fourteen in every school. The policy options for supporting families with very young children will require significant public investment and need to be addressed in the Comprehensive Spending Review in 2007.

This chapter explains why universal services are important, sets out the challenge of delivering childcare for all three to fourteen year olds, assesses the public policy options for supporting children under the age of three and explains why reform and investment in the childcare workforce is essential if there are to be sufficient staff with the appropriate training to provide quality childcare services. A series of recommendations is set out at the end of this chapter.

Targeted programmes to universal provision

The Government has taken an important step towards universal provision with its commitment to provide childcare for all children aged three to fourteen. While the Government has made good progress in delivering the National Childcare Strategy, there are still significant gaps in the provision of affordable, high quality and accessible childcare across the country, particularly for children under the age of three. Targeted programmes by definition do not reach all children. While there are 500 SureStart programmes in the poorest parts of the UK, they only cover an estimated one third of children under four living in poverty.[1] Children with disabilities and children with a parent who is disabled have not benefited from new childcare places. Parents who have a child with a disability are seven times less likely to be in paid employment, and childcare for disabled children can be prohibitively expensive due to the increased ratio of staff to children required.[2] A universal childcare service must provide clear entitlements for children with disabilities, and services must be accessible.

Many parents struggle to afford childcare, particularly those living in London. The Daycare Trust's 2004 Childcare Costs Survey found that the average cost for a full-time nursery place for a child under two is £134 a week, almost £7000 a year, with the cost rising to an average of £168 per week or £8736 per year in inner London. The current average award through the childcare element of the Working Tax Credit is £40.69 per week which is less than a third of the average cost of a nursery place. The Government needs to provide additional funding for childcare in London as the thresholds for the tax credits are too low, particularly for places for under threes or for families with two or three children, and as a consequence London has the highest child poverty rates in the UK. Large families are more likely to be living in poverty than families with one or two children, yet they do not receive extra financial support for childcare. The Working Tax Credit needs to be reformed to increase the threshold of financial support available to large families, so as not to disadvantage children who have several brothers and sisters.

The Government will not be able to abolish child poverty by 2020 unless it provides services which all children living in low income households can access, regardless of whether their parents are in work or where they live. There are also other significant advantages from developing services that can be used by all families. Children, particularly those from disadvantaged families, thrive from interacting with children from a variety of different backgrounds. Services used by middle class families have greater public support and are less likely to be closed when funding is restricted. The provision of universal childcare for three to fourteen year olds is a major opportunity to build public support for investing in childcare, which will be important when the Government comes to decide on services for families with very young children, where the options are more expensive.

Delivering for all children aged 3 to 14

Providing all children aged between three and fourteen with quality childcare will require long-term funding, the recruitment and training of new staff, strengthening the leadership and management capacity of schools to provide services for 52 weeks of the year, and working in partnership with the NHS and social services. Schools which offer breakfast and after-school clubs support them from a myriad of funding streams, including charging parents. There are far too many uncoordinated childcare programmes with separate funding streams, planning and bidding processes and targets, which makes planning services impossible.[3] The NHS could never have been established on a cocktail of short-term funding streams; now is the time to provide schools with long-term revenue funding to develop childcare services.

The Government needs to decide whether all three and four year olds will be entitled to free full-time nursery education (9am to 3.30pm) or whether they will continue to receive free part-time places (two and a half hours a day). Should parents who need full-time provision from 8am to 6pm pay for a morning or afternoon session of nursery education, as well as the childcare element of the day? It is unclear how the development of new school based services will fit with the development of new Neighbourhood Nurseries, many of which will be run by private providers, as their viability may depend upon having a proportion of pre-school children using their services. Schools will need to develop their workforce as play schemes and holiday programmes have been run by staff with few qualifications and little training, on low hourly rates of pay.

As well as running holiday programmes, schools should be encouraged to consult parents and children about offering weekend programmes, including whole-family activities. Many children and young people would like to take part in music, drama, art and sports at the weekend but cannot do so either because the activities are not available or because they are too expensive. Children also need support at the weekends, particularly if one or both of their parents are working, which is the situation in the majority of two and one parent families.[4] Providing all children with after-school childcare will give them new opportunities in a safe environment whilst enabling their parents to balance their work and family responsibilities. This should make a significant difference to lone parents' career opportunities.

Supporting families with very young children

Very young children are more expensive to care for than older children, and any of the policy options facing the Government in this area will require significant investment of public money. Yet increasing support for families in the very early stages of a child's life will significantly alleviate the impact of poverty and poor parenting on their development. The starting point in developing services for families should be the evidence on child development and the views of parents on how they would like their child to be cared for during its first years of life.

The quality of parents' and carers' interactions with children has a critical impact upon children's cognitive, social and emotional development.[5] The amount of verbal interaction parents have with their children has been shown to influence language development and reading ability during later childhood, the effects of which may persist into adult life. Furthermore, children with more secure parental attachments appear less likely to be socially isolated and aggressive in pre-school and school.[6] The overriding public policy objective must therefore be to give parents greater support in providing a secure, nurturing environment for their children, particularly in their early years of life. This should include the provision of high quality, affordable childcare, but also greater support for parents who want to look after their children on a part-time or full-time basis.

Given the importance of how parents and carers interact with babies and toddlers, public policy should take account of the findings of research studies on the impact of different types of childcare. The evidence suggests that nurseries may not necessarily be the best form of care for very young children, particularly if their parents work full-time, unless it is of the highest quality. The rationale underpinning this assessment is that the development of very young children depends upon receiving loving and nurturing care from people who know them well. Nurseries with a qualified and stable staff team will provide higher quality care than those nurseries which employ unqualified childcare workers and agency staff. Staff turnover is therefore a critical factor in determining the quality of care provided to very young children. It should be of major concern to policy-makers that staff turnover in childcare services is high: 23 per cent of nurseries and 16 per cent of out of school clubs had vacancies in 2001.[7] In Ofsted's second annual report on early years inspections in England, 51 per cent of nurseries were rated as 'good' while 48 per cent were rated as 'satisfactory'. The Government needs to drive up standards so all nurseries are rated as 'good' or 'excellent' by improving staff training and remuneration.

Improving the quality of nursery care, especially for young children, should be as important as expanding provision.

Many parents will want to combine looking after their children with paid employment, but feel that their options are restricted by the low rate of maternity pay and the high cost of childcare for children under the age of three. While the Government has introduced the right to request flexible working and reforms to maternity and paternity leave, it does not give the majority of parents genuine choice about whether to return to work during the first year of a child's life. While mothers can take up to a year's maternity leave, the second six months is unpaid. As a consequence, some mothers return to work earlier than they would wish because they cannot afford the loss of family income. Other parents would like to return to work but cannot do so because they cannot find good quality affordable childcare that meets their needs.

The public policy choices open to the Government include providing a range of family support services and activities for all parents and children such as home visiting and parent and toddler groups; increasing the public subsidy for childcare for under threes on an income-related basis; and funding maternity leave at a higher level and paid parental leave on an income-related basis. All three could be achieved with public support for greater investment in children's services, but it will take time to recruit and train staff and establish new services. Given what is known about early childhood development and the importance of support for parents, the priority in the next Comprehensive Spending Review should be to pay maternity leave at a higher rate for six months, to introduce paid parental leave and provide a range of services for all parents and children on the SureStart model.

The Government will need to decide on the extent to which it can afford to subsidise childcare costs both for low income families on benefits and for all families on an income-related basis. The case for greater public investment is compelling: a universal childcare and early years service would reduce child poverty, improve educational achievement and enable parents to combine their family responsibilities with work or study. A recent report estimated that the annual £15 billion cost would be offset by increased parental employment and better prospects for children.[8] Nevertheless, the challenge facing the Government is that while there will be long term savings from investing in children's services, additional investment will be required at a time when economic growth has slowed down. This will raise difficult issues about choices in public spending and whether to raise taxes to pay for new childcare services at a time when there is pressure to increase investment in pensions and transport.

The decisions that the Government makes on investment in childcare will determine whether it succeeds in eradicating child poverty by 2020. The New Deal for Lone Parent programme, tax credits and affordable childcare have increased the proportion of lone parents in employment since 1997. For the Government to achieve its target of 70 per cent of lone parents in employment, it will need to provide more intensive support to those parents who are on benefits.

Lone parents claiming benefits are more likely to have difficulty with basic skills, have limited experience of work and have three or more children, than those who have found work since 1997. Research commissioned by the DfES found that 78 per cent of non-working lone mothers said they would prefer to go out to work or study if they had access to good quality, convenient, reliable and affordable childcare.[9] There is evidence that for lone parents, the gains from moving off benefits and into paid work are low. Once the childcare costs are taken into account, the lone parent may be worse off.[10] However, the availability of childcare is not the only factor which influences lone parents' decisions to seek paid work. The New Deal for Lone Parents evaluation found that 53 per cent of non-working lone parents said that they did not want to leave their child with anyone else. If the alternative is working long hours for low pay including shift work, it is understandable that mothers want to be at home with their children.

Although participation in New Deal for Lone Parents is optional for parents with children under the age of five, the Government will need to decide whether it wants to target funding for childcare to increasing the subsidy to parents going back to work with very young children. The childcare costs of a baby can easily represent half a lone parent's salary. An alternative approach would be to provide higher child benefit for very young children, support with parenting and childcare places for lone parents who need to improve their skills and qualifications before seeking employment once their youngest child is three and eligible for a nursery place at primary school.

To provide more childcare places the Government will need to embark upon a major reform of the childcare workforce to provide sufficient staff with the appropriate training to run new services.

Reform of the childcare workforce

The quality of childcare services is directly linked to the skills, experience and remuneration of the childcare workforce.[11] While nursery teachers share the same terms and conditions as school teachers, other early years workers endure low pay and poor conditions of service, and many are still inadequately trained. In 2003, the average salary for childcare staff paid annually was £6,100 and for those staff paid hourly it was £5.50 per hour.[12] Unsurprisingly, the sector suffers from serious difficulties in recruiting and retaining staff. Staff shortages are likely to get worse, as the childcare sector competes for staff with education, social services and the NHS, as well as with the private sector. As the majority of young people at university are now women, they will have access to a much wider range of employment opportunities and are unlikely to choose to work in low paid, low status jobs such as childcare. It should be a source of shame that women with low qualifications can earn more money working in supermarkets than caring for young children.

Reforming the childcare workforce in the UK would involve increasing the proportion of graduates and people with level 3 qualifications working with young children. This cannot be achieved without paying higher salaries and making working with children attractive to men. In Denmark the majority of nursery workers are 'pedagogues', who have degree level training, compared with a two year post-16 training course in the UK. Danish pedagogues earn approximately twice as much as childcare workers in the UK.

The public policy dilemma facing the Government is that parents in the UK already pay around 75 per cent of childcare costs, significantly higher than in most OECD countries. Yet investment is essential to expand and improve the quality of services and to deliver genuinely integrated children's services. This tension is only likely be resolved by sustained public investment in early years services. As a nation, Britain spends 0.2 per cent of GDP on childcare and early years compared with 2 per cent in Denmark.[13] Very few employers subsidise their employees' childcare costs and this is unlikely to change in the future unless they face major recruitment challenges, as in the NHS.

While no one would underestimate the political challenges of confronting difficult choices about the balance of taxation and public expenditure, there are significant costs in not investing in developing the skills and expertise of people working with children. In 1968 the Seebohm reforms created Social Services Departments in what was seen as a 'great leap forward' for personal social services.[14] The vision articulated by Seebohm was never realised, a major contributory factor being the failure to invest in workforce development; it has only in the last ten years become a requirement to undertake a three year degree to become a social worker. Reform of the childcare workforce is the most pressing issue facing the Government if it is to translate its vision into reality for parents and children. Yet by investing in the childcare workforce, the Government will also achieve another major objective, that of closing the gender pay gap. For too long our public services have relied on low paid women workers to sustain them.

Conclusion

How we care for young children conveys a powerful message about the type of society Labour Governments want to create in twenty-first-century Britain. Services which are used by all sections of the community help to foster a more socially cohesive society as well as transforming the opportunities for children and parents whose lives are blighted by disadvantage and poverty. The Government has an unprecedented opportunity to build on the success of SureStart by developing a universal childcare and early years service in the same way as the 1945 Labour Government created the NHS. Only a small minority of parents will ever be able to afford the full cost of childcare, so long term public funding is essential if all children are to have an equal start in life.

How to create a universal service

— Provide all children aged three and four with five hours free nursery education per day during term time as part of the Government's commitment to extended schools for all three to fourteen year olds.

— Ensure that all new childcare and play facilities are fully accessible to children with disabilities and make funding available to adapt existing premises.

— Provide all children with disabilities and children who have a parent with a disability with a number of free hours of childcare per week.

— Encourage schools to consult parents about providing childcare services at the weekend for working parents and during the holidays.

— Improve the quality of childcare services so 80 per cent of nurseries and childminders are rated as excellent or good by OFSTED.

— Increase levels of maternity pay and introduce payment for parental leave on an earnings-related basis.

— Provide a range of family support services and activities for children for families with children aged three and under in every neighbourhood.

— Ensure that all lone parents on benefits with children under three are able to access a childcare place to enable them to improve their skills and qualifications.

— Establish an Early Years and Childcare Leadership and Management Centre to develop future leaders and managers of children's centres, extended schools and Children's Trusts.

— Reform the early years and childcare workforce to create a career structure for all staff working with children, a qualifications framework (from entry level to masters' qualifications) and improved pay and conditions. Working with children to become a 'profession' like teaching, nursing and medicine.
— Recruit more men and graduates to the early years and childcare profession.
— Develop a long-term funding strategy for childcare and early years services, including subsidizing childcare places for children aged three and under.
— Integrate funding streams for childcare into a single budget to be managed at a local level by Children's Trusts.
— Reform the childcare element of the Working Tax Credit to provide greater financial assistance to families with more than two children and to reflect the higher costs of childcare for children aged three and under.
— Provide additional funding for childcare in London where costs are greater than in other parts of the UK.

References

1. Lisa Harker and Liz Kendall, *An Equal Start: Improving Support During Pregnancy and the First 12 Months* (IPPR, 2003).
2. Strategy Unit, Cabinet Office, *Inter-Departmental Childcare Review – Delivering for children and families* (November 2002).
3. *Ibid.*; National Audit Office, *Early Years – Progress in Developing High Quality Childcare and Early Years Education Accessible to all* (London: Stationery Office, 2004).
4. La Valle, I., et al, *Happy Families? Atypical Work and its Influence on Family Life* (Joseph Rowntree Foundation, 2002).
5. Edward Melhuish, 'Child Benefits: The Importance of Investing in Quality Childcare', *Facing the Future*, 9 (Daycare Trust, 2004); Sue Gerhardt, *Why Love Matters: How Affection Shapes a Baby's Brain* (London: Routledge, 2004).
6. *An Equal Start*.
7. Woodland, S., Miller, M., and Tipping, S., *Repeat Study of Parents' Demand for Childcare*, Research Report 348 (DfES, 2002).

8. *Universal Early Education and Care in 2002: Costs, Benefits and Funding Options* (Daycare Trust 2004); Alakeson, V., 'A 2020 Vision for Early Years: Extending Choice; Improving Life Chances', *Leading the Vision* 2 (Social Market Foundation, 2004).

9. *Repeat Study of Parents' Demand for Childcare.*

10. 'Childcare for Working Parents', Fifth Report of Session 2002-03, Volume 1, House of Commons Work and Pensions Committee.

11. Moss, P., 'Beyond Caring—The Case for Reforming the Childcare and Early Years Workforce', *Facing the Future* 5 (Daycare Trust, 2003).

12. *Universal Early Education and Care.*

13. *Creating Opportunities, Building Futures,* Children Policy Manifesto (2004).

14. Timmins, N., *The Five Giants — A Biography of the Welfare State* (London: HarperCollins, 2004).

4 | Positive Parenting and the State
Phil Hope and Hetty Einzig

It's difficult for my mum & Dad they have to do the cooking, vicomeing,
Gardening, Pay money for me & Christmas presants.

Becky, 9

The family has been called the smallest democracy. It is the most influential arena of decision-making for children, where they first experience their rights and responsibilities, find out whether their expectations will be met and discover that their actions have consequences. It is within the family that children first develop vital skills of negotiation, sharing and conflict resolution. Positive parenting promotes such skills, which help individual children thrive and, as they grow up, add to the social capital of the whole community.

There is no such thing as the ideal parent. A 'nanny state' that attempts to impose a model of perfect parenthood will not succeed because there is no such model. Moreover, blaming parents for their children's failings without offering solutions leaves families less, not more, able to cope. The traditional view, that parents' behaviour is solely responsible for the way the child turns out, has dominated debate and policy development on the family for decades. Coupled with the belief that the family is a wholly private institution, this has led to public services for families being geared primarily to crisis intervention.

In turn this has created a climate of blame, and resulted in a neglect of policies that offer support to all parents.[1]

Having and bringing up children is not just a private business, a 'lifestyle choice'. Each family has too much impact on others, and the state, for good or ill, already plays a significant role in family life. The debate on family policy must therefore address the complexity of family dynamics, families' needs and interactions and the contribution they make to society. To shy away from acknowledging the role of the state is to ignore what happens already, and miss a vital part of what both families and family policy need.

We now know that a child's development is directly affected by an amalgam of genes, parenting, peers and the wider culture.[2] So we need policies on the family that are rooted in an understanding of the interactive and interdependent nature of family life, both between family members and between them and society.

Positive parenting

Many factors will contribute to the development of the child. It is however the primary relationships with parents and other key carers which in the first 6-12 months largely determine the 'internal map' of the child.[3] Lifelong and Family Learning initiatives recognize that the home is an effective learning environment for all. Nature is shaped through nurture: essential neurological wiring of the child is created through the give and take of these relationships. The parent is the child's first teacher (and, as many parents recognise, the child is also the teacher of the parent).

As children grow it is principally through these key relationships that they learn to understand themselves and relate to others. If cared for with love, attention and understanding, children will develop self esteem (a sense of their right to be), self awareness and, progressively, awareness of others. They will learn how to manage their own needs, passions and stresses, to self motivate, to nurture and to engage with others, and to take responsibility for their actions. This ability to relate lies at the foundation of a sense of well-being and of a sense of agency - and thus of being an active citizen.

These interpersonal skills for creating good relationships apply at work, in the home and in the neighbourhood. They include the ability to give and receive trust, build and sustain relationships, practise reciprocity, understand boundaries, be self-confident, manage powerful feelings, communicate, demonstrate reliability and work in a team. This 'emotional literacy' is more difficult to attain later in life. This is partly because we learn more easily and quickly when young, but also because it involves both heart and mind, and the best place to learn how to utilize both is within a loving environment, usually the family. Research shows that it is emotional intelligence, more than IQ, which has the greatest impact on life success.[4]

Just as positive parenting promotes emotional literacy, so unhelpful parenting practices are strongly associated with a range of negative outcomes for children, and self destructive or anti-social behaviour.[5] Children who do not have positive interactions with their parents are twice as likely to show persistent behaviour problems as those who do.[6] Hostile parenting style has a more negative impact on children and their behaviour than other factors such as income or family structure. Serious behavioural problems in childhood often lead to anti-social adult behaviour; this in turn is transmitted to the children of the future.[7] But there is now a wealth of evidence on positive parenting styles that promote better outcomes for children. We know that providing help and support for parents, and in particular the learning opportunities to reflect, understand and gain new skills, can enhance parent-child relationships, reduce anti-social behaviour in children and break the inter-generational cycles of emotional deprivation.[8]

The wider benefits of better parenting

Improving parenting skills can bring direct financial benefits to the whole community. We see around us how anti-social behaviour by children imposes considerable costs, which lead to higher public expenditure. Unaddressed, this behaviour leads to greater personal distress and greater costs to the public purse by the time those children reach adulthood. The accumulated financial costs—in terms of health care, crime management and special needs—of 27-year-olds who had conduct disorders in childhood is ten times greater than for those who did not have childhood behavioural problems. Antisocial behaviour in childhood is a major predictor of how much an individual will cost society, and a far more reliable indicator than parental social class.[9] There are real and substantial savings in public expenditure to be made from investing in parents and their children before serious problems arise.[10]

The benefits of supporting parents go wider than the individual child. Social capital refers to the levels of trust, belonging, co-operation and participation in community affairs that exist in networks of social relations between families within a community. The links between individuals and communities with high social capital and other positive outcomes such as good health and sustained employment is well documented.[11] Social capital is not fixed but is directly influenced by changes in the behaviour of individuals in the community.[12] Building social capital within communities, particularly in the most deprived areas, is a critical factor in sustained regeneration.

Parents have a particularly high personal investment in creating a secure, healthy community. They, more than anyone, want a safe and pleasant place in which children can grow up. We know that participating in a parenting group enhances parents' self-confidence to do other things in their lives—further education for example.[13] Groups often form strong networks and together are motivated to make changes to the community they live in. The skills they acquire in order to develop positive relationships with their children are the same skills they need to build and invest in their communities.[14]

If more people start to participate in anti-social activities in a community then we might expect social capital to decline. It follows that if relationships within the family and social relations within the community improve then social capital might increase and sustainable regeneration be more likely. Just as young people need the ability to form a vision for their future and identify goals and targets to achieve this, to give them the hope and enthusiasm to engage with society, so the birth of a child provides the opportunity to parents of any age to re-address these same processes. Planning for the future of one's child involves thinking about one's own life afresh. The best parenting education programmes and support initiatives provide these opportunities – often leading to raised expectations and a re-engagement with a range of social activities.

The most successful organisations pay a lot of attention to the quality of relationships in the workplace because it improves their bottom line. We need to do the same to improve the quality of life for people in our communities. We will not break the cycle of intergenerational deprivation that perpetuates poverty, ill health, underachievement and antisocial behaviour without measures to strengthen family and community relationships.

Better relationships won't in themselves eliminate poverty. Children are living in poverty because their parents are poor, and a decent income for parents through employment is the primary need to be met. Parents who are on very low incomes have to cope with more than just not having enough money. They inevitably find it hard to lift themselves out of poverty because of their own low expectations, low levels of academic achievement and low self esteem. These characteristics are often rooted in the relationships they had as they grew up. Often they were raised by parents who themselves suffered from negative parenting. The task of eliminating poverty requires that we include parenting education and support for the poorest parents as a key element in breaking that cycle.

Support for all parents

It is entirely appropriate that programmes such as SureStart, New Deal for Communities, Neighbourhood Renewal Areas and the Children's Fund should have begun life in the most disadvantaged areas. However we should now be mainstreaming the good practice that area-based family initiatives have developed. Such initiatives have the potential to be expanded so that every parent and child can benefit whatever their circumstances and wherever they live. The principle of progressive universalism suggests that we should target help on those who need it most, but also promote parenting education as a service for all parents.

In 2003 a pilot scheme to provide information sessions to parents at a time of key transitions in their children's lives (school transfers, GCSE year) proved very successful. This approach was piloted and evaluated in three areas and has shown the value of providing parents with information and advice on parenting and child development for children at different ages. The feedback from the parents and the various agencies taking part was highly favourable and the immediate and medium term impacts were significant.[15]

Strong relationships are primarily, but not solely, forged in childhood. It is harder to put right later what has gone wrong at an early stage, but the teenage years are a time when parents are looking for help and a significant impact can be made on young people's development. Parenting Orders have proved to be successful in helping the parents of teenagers who commit offences, and are valued by the participants who only wish they could have had such help earlier.[16] But should all parents of adolescents have the offer of advice and support?

There is a strong case for creating the adolescent equivalent of SureStart for parents of older young people. Parents who are worried about the behaviour or moods of their teenage son or daughter would welcome having a place or a person to whom they could turn for information, advice or support. This should not be an expensive service of new buildings or facilities, but rather a well-trained network of parenting mentors and facilitators based in existing services like SureStart, or local secondary schools or adult education colleges, working with parents of teenagers individually or in groups in local communities. These parent-support workers or mentors would provide a back up service to support parents whose teenaged children are causing them anxiety. Could a teenage SureStart—call it 'Sure

Progress' — be a significant area for policy development in Labour's third term?

Working with fathers

For most people the word 'parent' is unconsciously taken to mean 'mother'. The influence of fathers and their potential for making a contribution to their children's lives are generally ignored. Fathers are treated as an optional extra if they are thought of at all. Recent high profile stunts have sought to draw attention to the inequality felt by some men in the access they are afforded to their children, but we are still awaiting a serious debate on the quality of paternal relationships.

Yet good father-child relationships are associated with an absence of emotional and behavioural difficulties in adolescence, greater academic motivation and less likelihood of being in trouble with the police.[17] Once fathers are involved they usually remain so throughout childhood. High positive father involvement at age seven is associated with higher educational attainment among girls and boys, and leads to more satisfactory marital relations later in life, especially for girls.[18]

Fathers do want to improve their parenting skills but are deterred from doing so by locations, activities and materials which are oriented towards mothers. If parenting education is to be effective, much greater attention needs to be paid to making it relevant and appealing to fathers.

Working with grandparents

The need to involve grandparents in any strategy for improving parenting skills is vital. Grandma or Nan often plays a huge part in the parenting patterns that exist within families — either guiding their daughter with bringing up a new baby or taking on that role directly themselves. Grandad might also be the only consistent male role model for many children. The importance of these relationships too has been long overlooked and understanding how they might be helping or possibly hindering the development of good parenting skills is an important area for further work. Some grandparents may, for example, need to relearn some parenting skills given the changes in the world around them.[19]

Support for marriage

Contrary to popular media myths, marriage as an institution is not under threat. A married couple in a loving and long term relationship has proved its worth as a structure for bringing up children. But we know that families come in all shapes and sizes — and they work! Ultimately research tells us that no particular family structure will guarantee the development of secure attachments or that the parenting needs of children are met. What is important is the nature and quality of the relationships within the family and the parenting of the children.[20] Again, awareness, mutual attentiveness and responsibility are key ingredients of success. It is these key relationships and supportive community networks that foster secure attachments and resilience. Supporting and educating parents in this role will help to build and sustain long term loving relationships — including marriage.

Conclusion: the empowering state

Labour has already made great strides in rehabilitating the concepts of family, community and society, and encouraging a lively discourse in these areas. The Government has already taken a number of important steps to provide parents with support, education and training. From the very start in 1997, Labour's Family Task Group mapped out a range of strategies for helping parents, including financial support for the poorest families, family-friendly employment measures and practical support for childcare. There is now a wide range of initiatives and funds to cover different aspects of families' lives — universal ante-natal and post-natal support, SureStart and children's centres, expanded childcare and nursery provision, direct financial support and the Children's Fund and Parenting Fund. Many of these programmes have now been brought together within the Children, Young People and Families

Division at the DfES, rather than being spread across a number of departments. This is a major advance; previous 'silo' thinking is being replaced by a holistic and collaborative approach.

But we have a way to go before parents truly feel that parenting — 'growing' the next generation on behalf of us all — is a valid and valued choice that can be combined with the world of work.[21] Supporting parents, improving parenting skills and strengthening personal relationships is done not just in order to prevent the worst happening to children in communities that experience the most disadvantage — though morally and financially that has been a good place to begin. It is also about a vision for the future of child-parent relationships in every family, and about building the social capital in every community to raise aspirations and achievement for all children and generations to come.

Crucially, parenting education is not about telling parents what to do — that doesn't work in practice and is not an appropriate role for the state in anything other than exceptional circumstances. Parenting education is about providing parents with information, advice when sought, and a range of supportive, learning opportunities that help them better understand and address the needs of their children and their own needs in order to enhance their relationships and life skills. But we must take care not to assume that support is an uncomplicated good: parents must have choice and they want to remain in control when dealing with their problems.[22] So it is the enabling and responsive state, not the nanny state, which enables children and their parents to fulfil their potential and make the very most of their lives to the benefit of themselves and the wider community.

If the first term of this Labour Government can be characterised as creating a strong and stable economy and the second term as strengthening high quality public services, then the next major task is to focus on supporting families and building sustainable communities. A major goal for Labour's third term must be to build on the work already made on the 'hardware' of society — better schools, homes and hospitals — and

49

focus upon strengthening the 'software' of society, the relationships that bind us together.

References

1. Pugh, G., De'Ath, E., Smith, C., *Confident Parents, Confident Children: Policy and Practice in Parent Education and Support* (London: National Children's Bureau, 1994).

2. Cowan, C.P., and Cowan, P.A., 'What an Intervention Design Reveals About how Parents Affect their Children's Academic Achievement and Behaviour Problems', in *Parenting and the Child's World: Influences on Academic, Intellectual and Socio-Emotional Development*, ed. Borkowski, J., Ramey., S., Bristol-Power, M., (New Jersey and London: Lawrence Erlbaum Associates, 2002).

3. Bowlby, J., *A Secure Base* (1988), cited in Park, J., 'The Emotional Education of Parents: Attachment Theory and Emotional Literacy', in *Parenting Education and Support: New Opportunities*, ed. Einzig, H., and Wolfendale, S., (London: David Fulton, 1999).

4. Goleman (1995), Emotional Intelligence. Bloomsbury, London.

5. Royal College of Paediatrics and Child Health, *Helpful Parenting: Report of a Joint Working Party* (London: RCPCH, 2002).

6. National Longitudinal Survey of Children and Youth, cycle 2 (Canada, 1996).

7. Scott, S., 'Aggressive Behaviour in Childhood', *British Medical Journal* 316 (1998), 202-6.

8. Einzig, H., 'Review of the Field: Current Trends, Concepts and Issues', in *Parenting Education and Support.*

9. Scott, S., Knapp, M., Henderson, J., Maughan, B., 'Financial Cost of Social Exclusion: Follow-up Study of Anti-social Children into Adulthood', *British Medical Journal* 323 (July 2001), 191.

10. Scott, S., Spender, Q., Doolan, M., Jacobs, B., Aspland, H., 'Is Childhood Antisocial Behaviour Treatable in Real Life? Multicentre Controlled Trial', *British Medical Journal* 323 (July 2001), 194.

11. Kawachi, I., Kennedy, B.P., Glass, R., 'Social Capital and Self-Rated Health: A Contextual Analysis', *American Journal of Public Health* 89 (1999), 1187-1193.

12. Robert Putnam, *Bowling Alone: The Collapse and Revival of American Community* (Simon & Schuster, 2000).

13. Samra, B., 'Supporting Parents Through Parenting Programmes', in *Parenting Education and Support*.

14. Einzig, H., Cowley, C., *SureStart Holloway: Consultation with Hard to Reach Parents*, conducted for the London Borough of Islington (London: Parenting Education and Support Forum, 2001).

15. Bhabra, S., and Ghate, D., *Parent Information Point: Evaluation of the Pilot Phase* (London, National Family and Parenting Institute, 2004).

16. Ghate, D., and Ramella, M., *Positive Parenting: The National Evaluation of the Youth Justice Board's Parenting Programme* (London: Youth Justice Board for England and Wales, 2002).

17. Flouri, E., and Buchanan, A., 'Father involvement and outcomes in adolescence and adulthood', End of Award Report (ref. R000223309) ESRC, 2001).

18. *Ibid.*

19. McNeill, F., 'You Don't Want to do it Like That', *The Guardian* (7 July 2004).

20. Cowan, C.P., and Cowan, P.A., *When Partners Become Parents: The Big Life Change for Couples* (USA Basic Books, 1992).

21. Bunting, M., *Willing Slaves: How the Overwork Culture is Ruling our Lives* (London: Harper Collins, 2004).

22. Quinton, D., *Supporting Parents: Messages from Research* (Jessica Kingsley, 2004).

5 | Economy-Friendly Families
Richard Reeves

*I think extended schools are good if the mother and father are both
working, you don't have to sit doing nothing, you can do activities and
things.*

Siobahn, 10

C hildren and economics mix like oil and water. Parents resort to
explaining that 'money doesn't grow on trees' in an attempt to
introduce the idea of fiscal prudence to their offspring. And
economists have largely ignored children, on the grounds that they
have limited consumer power (though pester power has been under-
rated), do not participate in the labour market and are, to boot,
frequently irrational.

Unlike the other social sciences—especially sociology and
psychology—economics has been an adults-only branch of the
academy. This deficit has become apparent in recent years, as the entry
(actually re-entry) of women into the labour market has put the
economics of reproduction onto the agenda. As the US economist
Shirley Burgraff puts it: 'Children might as well come from cabbage
patches as far as most political and economic theory is concerned.'[1] But
the largely successful assault by women on the labour market has
changed the political economy of childcare beyond recognition.
Previously the labour market was built on a 'buy one, get one free
model'. In Burgraff's words: 'The fact [is] that there used to be millions

of invisible employees. Employers who once got two (an employee with a backup spouse at home) are now most often getting just one.' The question of how we raise the next generation is therefore no longer a familial and social issue: it is now a vital economic one too.

We are at a crossroads. The gains made by women at work have come at a price in terms of family life: a truth which conservatives are attempting to exploit and progressives trying hard to ignore. But hard questions confront us as social democrats, who refuse to see the solution to our current problems lying in nostalgia for a housewifely past.

The goal of putting children higher up the economic agenda – of creating a truly 'child-friendly economy' – is an ambitious one. But if social democracy is to mean anything, it has to mean improving the wellbeing, security and life chances of children. And there are a number of positive steps which can and should be taken by the state and other institutions. But no real progress is possible unless we are willing to ask and answer some tough questions, of which two stand out.

First, to what extent has the take-up of paid work by women undermined family life – and in particular, the successful raising of children? Second, at what point is greater support for parents through the labour market inimical to economic productivity? In other words, how far does the so-called 'win-win' really extend?

There is no questioning the enormous benefits that have flowed from the dramatic rise in the number of women in the labour market, for the economy, for family income and of course for women themselves. There has been nothing short of a revolution in women's life chances. It is true that the labour market is far from a feminine citadel; the most senior positions are still hogged by men, the pay gap is stubbornly stuck at about 80 per cent and occupational segregation is still market. But women now fill a third of management positions and half the work-force.[2]

The significance of the greater range of choices available to women, and their greater financial independence, cannot be overstated. And the benefit to the economy of a bigger and better labour force is obvious.

53

But on the other side of the coin, the departure of women from the full-time work of childrearing and home-making has left a gap with contours which are much harder to measure. As Burgraff points out, the benefits of increased female employment are tangible, and measurable in economic terms, while the costs are largely invisible. Because the unpaid work done by women was never captured by the economists — and probably never fully could be — we can't even guess at the size of the loss.

There is some evidence that children who are in nurseries from a young age suffer some behavioural difficulties, and separate work suggesting a deterioration in adolescent mental health. This is rightly an area of considerable controversy, not least in feminist circles. But there is now too much empirical evidence suggesting that parents might be the best people to look after their young children to be ignored, or dismissed as conservative fantasy.

But even if children are paying a price for their mothers' advancement, this is not to suggest that it is greater than the gains in terms of equality and productivity. Children do not always hold the trump card. Nor is the remedy simply a reversal of recent trends to greater working equality: even if this were possible (imagine the posters — Women: Your Children Need You), it would be utterly regressive. But it is necessary for social democrats to recognise that the huge improvement in opportunities for women may have come with some side-effects.

These potential costs for children would have been less if the labour market had changed as much as women have. For all the talk of the 'feminisation' of the workplace, the nature of jobs, the culture of organisations and benchmarks of success have remained largely undented. As Heather Hopfl has put it, women have often succeeded as 'quasi-men'.[3] Women have therefore been faced with much harder choices than men, not least between career and family. The overwhelming majority of male CEOs have children; most female CEOs do not. And the adoption by many women of traditionally male working patterns has added to the pressure on the family. So far we have seen, in terms of working life, less a feminisation of work than a masculinisation of women. 'The majority now absolutely believes that women can do what men can do,' says Gloria Steinem. 'The next step is to believe that men can do what women can do.'

At the same time, many governments, not least the New Labour administrations, have been keen to encourage or cajole single mothers into the labour market. The social and economic case for these policies is strong; paid work is indeed the surest route out of poverty. But some of the political rhetoric has contributed to a perception that it is family life that needs reform, rather than the workplace.

Recent announcements that schools are to offer 'all-day opening' to allow parents to work more easily are in a similar vein. The assumption is that parents should be in paid work (and indeed most do want to be); that the jobs will be of a traditional, full-time nature; and that educational and childcare institutions must be built around these realities. All of these trends, taken together, mean that rather than creating a family-friendly economy we are busily creating economy-friendly families.

The second hard question is the trade-off between family-friendliness and economic efficiency. The official progressive line is that by offering greater support for families, businesses will benefit from more loyal and motivated employees and that there is therefore no trade-off between social and economic objectives. This argument is certainly true, up to a point. But the competitive advantages to individual firms disappear once all firms fall into, or are regulated into, line. And the costs of providing more generous leave, or even managing multiple parental absences are real. *The Daily Mail*, CBI and Federation of Small Businesses can be relied on to proclaim the imminent collapse of capitalism if the modest package suggested by Patricia Hewitt is enacted; the TUC, government and pressure groups can be relied on to suggest that competitiveness will be unaffected, or even enhanced.

The work done by the LSE's Catherine Hakim on the Swedish labour market suggests that the truth lies somewhere in the middle.[4] She points out that the generosity of maternity benefits in that social democratic utopia have hardened the segregation of the labour market. Three-quarters of employed women are in the public sector while three-quarters of men are in the private sector — because firms in competitive markets are less likely to be able to afford the generous maternity packages available. From an equality point of view, this has obvious negative consequences, not least because public sector wages are lower. (In the Darwinian US labour market the pay gap is much smaller.) But there is a deeper significance to Hakim's work: the fact that family-friendliness inevitably eventually collides with competitiveness, especially in tradeable goods and services.

It is not clear that the UK has reached, or is even close to that collision. Certainly the improvements introduced in the first two Labour terms appear to have had no negative impact. But a serious social democratic programme has to allow for the fact that in economic terms, family-friendliness may not be a free lunch. Having repeatedly made the 'business case' for reform, we now need to start making the broader social and moral case with more vigour.

The need for a new social democratic approach to family and work is pressing, and not just because of the challenges already outlined. There is a political danger too. The Conservative plans to offer some financial reward to parents (for which read mothers) to stay at home with their children may begin to strike a chord with a generation which takes seriously the evidence on child development and rejects the Jurassic structures of most employing organisations. Thus far, Labour has pursued a largely economistic route, based on helping get wages to women. This approach is reaching both its policy and political limits. We now need to find an alternative to either simply making families market-ready or attempting to turn back the clock.

The good news is that there are some senior politicians willing to wade into this turbulent water. Patricia Hewitt, in particular, understands the complexities of the challenge both from a policy and human perspective (she has said her greatest regret is not taking more time off to spend with her young children). Her reforms to date, and those suggested in her recent IPPR pamphlet, show that she is determined to nudge UK employers into policies around leave and flexibility which they are unlikely to come to themselves.[5] The most important shift in recent years has been the explicit recognition that greater equality at work requires greater equality at home — that men's lives now need to change if women are to secure their hard-won gains. As Michael Kimmel has written: 'The second half of the transformation of gender is just beginning, and will be, I suspect, far more difficult to accomplish than the first. That's because there was an intuitively obvious ethical imperative attached to enlarging the opportunities for and eliminating the discrimination against women. But the transformation of the twenty-first century involves the transformation of men's lives.'[6]

The business lobby is vehemently opposed to improvements in paternity leave, and so the proposals in this area are an important signal of the Government's priorities: to make the two weeks leave payable at 90 per cent of salary, and the option to make the second six months of leave transferable to fathers. For every dad in a Batman suit, there are a million trying to raise a family with their partner — Labour needs to be on their side.

Beyond another package of reforms to improve maternity and paternity leave — surely welcome — Labour has to begin articulating a new approach based on four pillars: choice; quality of work; new success measures; and parental responsibility. Not all of these are amenable to state action or indeed principally a responsibility of government. But progressive leaders should always see their role as helping to point to alternative ways ahead, even if — perhaps especially if — they cannot force us down them.

Choice

The starting principle must be that families themselves are best placed to judge how to manage their affairs, and that the job of government is to maximise their choices. This means, for example, not pre-judging whether mothers or fathers should be principal carer (which current policy continues to do, although there are some moves in the right direction). It means giving equal support to parents who want to raise children themselves as to those who want to enter paid work and use paid childcare. This means offering parents a choice about whether to use state support to subsidise work, or childcare, or to stay at home themselves.

But a commitment to choice also means resisting calls for strict limits on working hours. It is not up to the state to tell us how many hours we may work—at least not if the liberal half of new Labour's 'liberal socialist' tag means anything. The best case for action to restrict working hours was made by John Stuart Mill in his *Political Economy*, on the basis that long working hours represent what economists now call a 'collective action problem'—in other words, a situation in which we would all choose shorter hours for all, but cannot as individuals bring this about. But as Mill suggests, 'the manner in which it would be most desirable that this effect should be brought about, would be by a quiet change in the general custom of the trade; short hours becoming, by spontaneous choice, the general practice'.[7]

Most people who work long hours do so of their own free will and enjoy their jobs. The self-employed work long hours—but say they have better work-life balance. And average working hours are trending downwards, a 'quiet change' in working patterns.

Quality of work

Parental working hours are in any case not the best measure of the way employment influences the wellbeing of children. Evidence from children themselves—especially in Ellen Galinsky's *Ask the Children*—suggests that what they most desire is that parents do not bring work stress home. There is a 'spillover' effect between work and home lives, in both directions. The quality of working life thus has a direct effect on the quality of family life. Parents doing a job offering respect, challenge, security, fair reward and a sense of achievement are better, more engaged, more energetic parents than those who feel trapped in lousy jobs which send them home frustrated or stressed. Gordon Brown once called for 'full and fulfilling' employment. So action on health and safety, employee consultation, discrimination and workplace bullying needs to be seen as part and parcel of good family policy.

New success measures
It may be that greater moves towards a child-friendly economy will be in opposition to a full-throated productivity drive. It is therefore essential to put economic growth and business productivity in perspective — to see them as important means to a better society, rather than as ends in themselves. Labour has often fallen into an economism which rests uneasily with a focus on the quality of life, not least for children. GDP growth continues to be brandished as a national medal of honour. But given that GDP growth probably contributes less and less to our sense of wellbeing, it is vital that social democrats develop and promote other, complementary, yardsticks of our social health too. As Robert Kennedy said of GDP: 'It does not allow for the health of our children, the quality of their education, or the joy of their play. It does not include the beauty of our poetry or the strength of our marriages, the intelligence of our public debates or the integrity of our public officials. It measures neither courage, nor our wisdom, nor our devotion to our country. It measures everything, in short, except that which makes life worthwhile.'

Against the benchmark of economic efficiency, child-friendliness will always struggle to score highly. But it is the wrong benchmark.

Shared responsibility
It is easy for centre-left commentators to blame 'the market' for the erosion of collective responsibility for children. But this is lazy thinking. The truth is that the market is neither anti-children nor pro-children: the wellbeing of children, and to a large extent adults too, is simply not captured, priced or traded in the market. It is an externality. And

59

markets are nothing if not responsive; if parents decided to put spending time with their children ahead of career success and material rewards, then they could. It is striking that families in which both parents work full-time are generally affluent: their labour market participation is not driven by economic need, in any meaningful sense. There can be little doubt that the values of consumerism, instant gratification and material acquisition are in direct conflict with the values of patience, sacrifice and nurturing which make for good child-rearing. But whose responsibility is it to realign our values? Government can take a lead, not least by example, and can make the choices of parents and carers easier. And Labour needs a dose of market scepticism.

But ultimately the creation of a child-friendly economy, and society, lies less in the hands of legislators than individuals, families and communities. It is instinctively harder, of course, for social democrats to recognise the limits of state power and instead engage in the more complex and controversial arena of value formation. But this is where the political action is increasingly likely to be. The shape of economies and markets depends less on government than on the demands and desires of citizens, workers and consumers. To that extent we get the economy we deserve.

References

1. Shirley Burgraf, *The Feminine Economy and Economic Man* (Reading, Mass: Perseus Books, 1998).

2. Equal Opportunities Commission, *Women and Men in Britain: Management* (2002).

3. Quoted in Michael Kimmel, *The Gendered Society* (Oxford: OUP, 2000).

4. Interview in *The Guardian* (22 September 2004).

5. Patricia Hewitt, *Unfinished Business* (London: Institute for Public Policy Research, 2004).

6. *The Gendered Society*.

7. John Stuart Mill, (1848/1995) *Principles of Political Economy*, Book V (University of Toronto Press, 1995), Chapter XI, pp.8-12.

"

6 | What are Children for Anyway?
Mary Riddell

The amount of pressure placed on parents by young children is something that I imagine must be hard to cope with.

Oliver, 18

Childhood moves many milestones. Each week, it seems, another record falls in the race to grow up. Or not to grow up. A boy of thirteen dies of heroin. Another, aged fourteen, commits suicide in a child jail. Both are billed as the youngest ever to meet these fates. In the champions' league of precocious suffering, being a child often seems hardly more than a brief prelude to the problems and despair of the adult universe.

Other barriers have been demolished, too. These are the hopeful results the government likes to stress. 700,000 children have been lifted out of poverty since 1997. A million childcare places have been created, and young people are the fulcrum of Labour's thinking. Placing children at the heart of third-term policy could not be more timely, or more artful. In a society grown jaded, fractious and afraid, politicians and voters can share a universal value. Everyone loves children.

This consensus cloaks a more nuanced reaction. Tap the words 'child-friendly society' into an internet search engine, and two curious entries head the results. The first is a site advising parents to start saving for their child's university education (cost, £7,011 per year), wedding

(£14,000) and first house (£121,000). The second is the home page of a family holiday company noted for its all-day childcare. While few would dispute that children cost a lot to bring up, or that parents like peace on the beach, the sub-text of both entries hints at how modern Britain sees the young: as expensive and burdensome.

Childhood is ringed by a forcefield of foreboding. Grown-ups are afraid of bad children, and fearful for good ones. Everyone wants their child not to be lonely, bullied, rejected or hurt. But such aspirations are part of a growing checklist of negative ambitions—that young people do not get seduced by chatroom predators or lipstick marketers; that they do not become obese or anorexic; that they are not denied a place at the best school or university; that they do not end up drunk, drugged, pregnant or dead. British children are among the safest in the world, and yet fear of risk is now so exaggerated that it causes dangers, rather than averting them. Withholding the MMR jab, for example, may damage many children while benefiting none.

If dreams are rationed, then so are the uses to which children can be put. Since we lack a market for under-age chimney sweeps and long ago gave up procreating out of social habit, it is customary to ask what children are for. The question is hackneyed, but the answer—beyond plugging tomorrow's pension gap—remains unclear. No one ever gave birth through altruism, and Britain, lacking selfish incentives to reproduce, has a birthrate plummeting along with much of the world's. The average number of children born to British women has fallen by a third in three decades, and one of four is likely never to have a baby. Most profess few regrets. Of those who do have a family, only 66 per cent of women and 41 per cent of men said their children made them 'most happy', according to a survey for Lever Faberge.

Society would be offended to think itself child-hostile, especially when worship of the young can border on the maudlin. We need to be clear, though, where this sentiment is focused. The grief unleashed when murder comes to Soham or Beslan is not simply sorrow for the executed. It is also a requiem for squandered innocence. Citizens can read, in the faces of Holly and Jessica and the burial pictures of Russian schoolchildren, an endorsement of old myths of childhood. These children, unchangeable as their peers grow old before their time, will not become drop-outs, or teenage rebels, or failures. They will never crush the fantasies of adults.

But childhood will not, and should not, become Alice Revisited. The spark for such nostalgia is the current crisis and confusion over children's lives. In seeking to put the young back at society's heart, the Government has many strategies, starting at the cradle. SureStart's 500 programmes have been rightly hailed as a success, although the scope is small. Childcare provision is improving—though still inadequate, with one place for every four children under the age of eight—and funding has been announced for 2500 children's centres by 2008, as well as 'wraparound' primary schools, open from 8am to 6pm. All three and four-year-olds have access to free part-time education, and, by 2005/06, spending on early years education and childcare will have tripled to £1.5 billion since 1997.

On the debit side, nursery workers are patchily trained and paid as little as £5.12 an hour. With such meagre wage rates, most daycare is not expensive, but it is often not affordable either. In London, some parents pay up to £344 a week to keep a two-year-old in nursery. Though the mantra is 'universalism', it is unclear how, and whether, the Treasury's targeting of poorer areas is going to be replaced (as it should be) with places for all and fees for those who can pay. The ten-year childcare review, unpublished at the time of writing, will reveal the full scope of the Government's ambition.

It seems axiomatic that babies should be offered the most equal start possible. But even before the dream of universal care is half-hatched, the backlash has begun, in media stories asserting that long (or even short) periods of nursery care for under-threes may be producing more insecure and aggressive children. Clearly, warehousing children is harmful. Equally, there is much evidence that good group care is beneficial even for the very young. The danger is that government may be tempted to

63

neglect daycare for the under-twos, thus condemning to sub-standard care, or poverty, many children whose parents need or want to work.

The upper end of childhood has its own problems. Teenagers are, supposedly, cracking up. A time trend study published in the *Journal of Child Psychology and Psychiatry* in November 2004 claimed that, by 1999, one in five girls had emotional problems and one in six boys was in trouble for bad behaviour. Depression is up 70 per cent since the mid-1980s, according to the study's researchers, whose findings coincided with newspaper reports about teenage suicide, self-harm, materialism, fecklessness and drinking binges.

Is the Government failing children? Are parents? Do nurseries incubate the tortured adolescents of tomorrow? What is really happening to children, and what should be done to make their lives better? How do parental responsibilities knit with those of the state? In answering those questions, it is necessary first to examine society's knack of alienating its young.

Few citizens are as darkly drawn as adolescents. The numbers of those out of their heads on Alcopops, or having unprotected sex with strangers, or gripped by despair, are inflated, often on dubious evidence, to an epidemic. We may love babies, but we demonise children who wear their vulnerability less fetchingly. Horror is reserved not just for those who, like James Bulger's killers, commit terrible crimes.

The fear of 'bad' children encourages government to bow to - and perhaps unwittingly to inflame — mob instinct at a time when teenagers continue to kill and harm themselves in custody. By November 2004, two under-17s had committed suicide in the state's care, as against none in the previous year. Only when victims like Joseph Scholes or Adam Rickwood are dead, and the soft faces and tragic stories emerge in the media, do we realise that it was all a case of mistaken identity. These boys, not our monsters but our victims, were only children after all.

Adolescents have always rebelled. St Augustine was a teenage shoplifter, and no one but an amnesiac would dismiss juvenile angst. The mistake is to treat older children as outsiders. Where do they get their miseries, their doubts, their surliness and their fixation with the material, if not from us? Far from being an alien breed, they are a mirror to the family, community, neighbourhood and nation that shaped them.

As John Coleman, of the Trust for the Study of Adolescence, says, it would be rash to deny that children, uncertain about their futures, are unhappy and possibly getting more so. Coleman thinks the pressures of fractured families are a factor. Though government cannot engineer stable homes, it can make the public realm more habitable. Instead, it risks deepening the divide between the 'good' child and the 'bad'.

Its principal emphasis is twofold: exam results and retribution. A levels or Asbos. Perversely, overly rigid education may be producing the very kind of child the government abhors — unhappy under-achievers more likely to end up in trouble. The number of students who drop out at 15 is among the highest in the developed world, according to an OECD report which places Britain 24th of 27. Slovakia has just overtaken us, and only Mexico, Portugal and Turkey have a worse record.

A total of 75.3 per cent of young people stay in education past 16, compared with 76.1 per cent the previous year. Conversely, 44 per cent of young people go on to university — close to the 50 per cent target. The test of Mike Tomlinson's blueprint for a new diploma system will not be the future of A levels but whether better vocational courses rescue the drop-outs of 16. If the Government is serious about helping teenagers with problems, it will also have to do as it suggested and finance its Connexions scheme to provide proper pastoral care rather than a pared-down service for the neediest.

Failure to spend money enough on children stems, in part, from their low status. Initiatives framed in their name are often devised with someone, or something, else in mind. The daycare strategy was evolved partly because it would benefit the economy if more mothers, especially single ones, went back to work. Had the focus been primarily on children, the Government would have realised (as it did, belatedly) that better leave and pay should also be provided to help parents stay at

65

home, if they wished, for a child's first year. Ministers might also have addressed the question of how the vast workforce needed for an expanding daycare service is to be found, trained and properly rewarded.

From early years to university, there is a vagueness about what government wants education to produce — well-rounded and thoughtful people, or cogs in the economy. What sort of citizens are we seeking to mould, and by what rules? In a wash of social and educational initiatives, the missing element is a unifying theory based on the best interests of the child.

For such a child-centred administration, Labour is coy to the point of omerta about young people's rights. The UN Convention on the Rights of the Child is the most universally accepted human rights prescription in history, and the least arid. Its articles cover happiness, love, understanding and freedom — the cornerstones of a good childhood. Every country in the world has signed it, bar America and Somalia. In Britain, it is perilously sidelined.

In September 2002, Cherie Booth QC accused the government of failing to live up to its obligations and predicted that the UN committee on the rights of the child would 'find the Government wanting in a number of respects, including juvenile justice, education, asylum-seekers and refugees.' The committee's report on UK compliance was duly critical, citing — among other reservations — the continuing legal right for parents to smack their children and the UK's unwillingness to raise its age of criminal responsibility.

Two years on, in the wake of Victoria Climbie's murder, the Children's Bill was designed to offer greater protection. While making significant advances in some areas, I believe it failed in two key respects to give children greater rights. A campaign to outlaw smacking failed after the Government refused a free vote on an amendment allowing equality under the law. Campaigners claim that the resulting compromise on light smacking is likely to offer children less protection than before. Secondly, members of all parties warned that the new Children's

Commissioner would be uniquely toothless. As Baroness Warnock asked the Government minister Lord Filkin: 'If we have accepted that there is such a thing as a human right, why is it impossible there is such a thing as a children's right? Children, after all, are human.'

Criminal responsibility remains set at ten, and eight in Scotland. At an age when many children are too young properly to join the threads of action and consequence, they are being publicly named and shamed. But it isn't just about the law. Britain also has trouble defining, in cultural terms, a coherent philosophy of childhood. As a consequence, children are treated simultaneously as fragile innocents, sexually-aware consumers or yobs and thugs. The infantile front men of Fathers4Justice get to dress up as Batman and Robin and fulfil fantasies of taking their complaint to Buckingham Palace, while small children are expected to be silently stoical about parental absence and divorce. Even the increasing, and welcome, emphasis on work/life balance and good parenting is seen through the prism of adult needs and rights.

Giving childhood back to children should start with two main policy measures, aside from alleviating child poverty. The first is a ban on smacking. Government obduracy will not prevent pressure for a move axiomatic both to children's safety and to showing that the most vulnerable citizens have the same rights as the strongest. The second step is to redraw the law so that no child of 14 and under is jailed or put on trial in an adversarial process designed for adults. Their cases, however serious, should be treated, as Baroness Helena Kennedy has argued, as matters of child welfare.

Older children, of 14 to 18, should also be placed in local authority care if on remand or found guilty of serious crimes. Around 3000 children aged between 15 and 17 are behind bars, despite evidence that child crime is falling. Young people, lonely, frightened, desolate and often convicted of nothing, continue to kill or harm themselves in alarming numbers. Adult society stares, mostly mutely, at the harsh treatment of the most deprived and most despairing. Ninety per cent of young people in prison are substance abusers or mentally ill.

67

They are not our children, society tells itself. But, of course, they are. If our children are threatened and vulnerable, so are these. If our children struggle with unhappiness and uncertainty, so do these. If our children have chased escape or oblivion in drink and drugs, so have these. They are not a travesty of modern childhood but the starkest illustration of the problems foisted on it. Their familiarity, not their otherness, explains why we are so afraid of them, and why we look away. In a society that makes monsters of young people, the solution for all children must begin with those deemed the most despicable.

But the neediest children do not tell the whole story. If young people are not deprived, then society has ways of making them so. An NOP survey published late in 2004 showed that a third of British children never go outside the home alone because of fears of abduction and murder (in reality a minuscule risk, unchanged in six years). These privileged prisoners gave disproportionate anxiety invested in them by a society terrified for some children and terrified by others.

Its remedies are excessive protection for the first group and undue punishment of the second. Asbos, which give rise to a criminal offence if breached, highlight the arrogance of a government that, despairing of bad families, uses legal muscle to place itself in loco parentis, forgetting that the state has usually proved the worst parent of all. Applying an Asbo costs £5000, according to the Crime and Society Foundation. Of those who break the order, a third end up in jail, at a price of £50,000 a year. This money would be far better spent on youth workers, on training police to deal better with young people and on the constructive activities, such as youth centres, that help prevent children turning to crime in the first place.

Making life better for young people means not only treating them better but liking them better, too. Creating a revolution of perception is not just a challenge for government. The campaigning magazine, *Young People Now*, points out that 70 per cent of press articles about children and teenagers are negative, and one in three reports are about crime. It's true. Look out for the stories about 'angels', illustrated by portraits of idealised children with polite smiles and hair damped down for school photographers. The subjects of such eulogies are almost invariably dead.

Obviously, many children have wonderful childhoods. They always did, and they always will, despite the strictures imposed by the adults of any generation. The latest burden, family breakdown, means upheavals, but not the 'timebomb' prophesied by the gloomy. Research suggests children are dealing quite well, and often benefiting, from complex families. In addition, it would be ludicrous to compare the lot of poorer children born in the twenty-first-century with their Victorian forebears. And yet, something is missing.

The Tory youth spokesman put his finger on the problem, admitting that, at the last election, his party 'didn't have a single policy developed with the needs and interests of young people first.' Labour has plenty, drawn from both ends of the spectrum; protection and punishment, carrot and stick. Many are ground-breaking and laudable. The problem, more fundamental a flaw than it ever seems, is that young people are curiously absent from the government debate. Like Hamelin in the wake of the Pied Piper's visit, there is hardly a child's voice to be heard.

Epilogue: Questions for Future Policy
Patrick Diamond and Meg Munn

The writers in this collection argue that an ideal society would be 'child-centred', a reflection of the egalitarian ethos and institutions of social democracy. It should not be surprising then that the Labour Party has spent a major period of its time in Government transfering resources to support children. The party after all was founded on the belief that it is the duty of Government not just to attack entrenched privilege, but to promote equality of life-chances across all spheres of life where it could exert influence.

Life-chances should be equalized as far as possible from the moment of birth. Social inequality is best tackled, and social mobility best advanced, if we deal with the causes at the root of injustice, before it becomes entrenched and inhibits the flowering of talent. Encouraging the nurturing of children within families helps the human personality to flourish in every sense. As A.H. Halsey reflected, 'the family is a socialist institution.'

Children are the future of communities and we have a duty to 'look after those on whom the future depends'. Individuals are much more than just self-interested economic agents. The socialist philosopher John McMurray once observed: 'We need each other to be ourselves.' Since 1997, the Labour Government has worked to correct the worst of Thatcherism—Britain's 'progressive deficit'. The challenge was to tackle a generation of chronic neglect and under-investment in the public sphere.

But solely focusing on the past limits our horizon—we need to entrench a progressive settlement in Britain that endures long after the present administration has left office. State-funded childcare is being cemented into the British welfare state as another 'untouchable' by any future government. Labour's childcare strategy—a million more child-care places already and affordable childcare for all by 2010—has not yet fully registered with voters, but as time passes it will become part of the 'public fabric' of society like the NHS.

There are strong indicators that family policy will be a key issue in the forthcoming general election. The Conservatives are examining policies to promote family values. Yet general platitudes will not do, and a rummage in the past history of the Conservatives' record will resonate badly with many voters. After eight years of Labour Government, however, the last Conservative administration may appear ancient history to many parents of young children. They just don't know what it would be like under a Conservative Government. Labour will there-fore take no family's support for granted.

Ten or fifteen years ago, children's policy was invariably a matter for female politicians. It simply failed to rank alongside the economy, defence, or the NHS as a 'proper' political issue. At that time, 30 per cent of people believed that 'it is a man's job to earn the money and a woman's job to look after the home and family'. Today, that figure has nearly halved to 17 per cent. As men have become increasingly involved in childcare responsibilities, these issues have moved from the political margins to the mainstream of public debate.

Recognising the individuality of families, work patterns, ages of chil-dren and existing support from extended family members, it is obvious that choice has to be central in supporting families through child care provision. Demonstrating that our policies offer real choice is critical. This has met some resistance from parts of the Labour party. They argue that choice is irrelevant to hospitals and schools; all people want is excellence in their own school or hospital. This mind-set ignores families' individual needs, and risks treating them as one homogenous entity — but life isn't like that!

Others try to paint extended school opening hours as 'warehousing for kids', 10 hours a day stacked on shelves. But opening up schools puts the power in the hands of parents, whether they want or need to use safe and convenient childcare in a school setting — with times to suit if they start work early in the morning or finish later in the evening.

Choice can only be available with sufficient capacity and diverse provision. Significant levels of investment are required. Prioritising that investment for parents who choose to stay at home with their children means fewer child minders, nurseries or extended schools for all.

There are still tough and challenging dilemmas, which this collection has sought to probe. It is intended to provide a stimulus to further debate and discussion on the centre-left about future policy priorities. These questions remain:

— To what extent is it possible to transform how markets and the economy are governed to promote the objectives of a child-friendly society?

— Is it possible to change personal behaviour within families beyond state benefits and income redistribution; what are the boundaries to the legitimate exercise of state power?

— Does international evidence suggest it is possible for governments to have a significant impact on long-term birth-rates — and does this matter?

— What can public policy do to prevent relationship breakdown, strengthen families, and minimize the risk of break ups — all in the interest of children?

— What are the trade-offs with other areas of public policy, for example the implications of transferring resources from older people to the young in an ageing society?

What is certain is that where childcare and the family were once regarded as dull and worthy, they are now being imbued with the excitement and moral meaning of political debate. This should not be surprising. No other social justice policy matters more for Britain's future.

Acknowledgements

The editors are extremely grateful to all the children and young people who gave their time to write, e-mail or talk about their views on childhood and parenting. They would also like to thank Jonathan Heawood at the Fabian Society for coordinating this project, Dennis Bates for his editorial input and Claire McCarthy for all her help and encouragement.